US TANK DEVELOPMENT

The United States was not one of the early pioneers of armoured warfare. The US Army only decided that it needed to adopt the tank after seeing British and French vehicles in action on the Western Front. The first US tank, the M1917, was a copy of the French Renault FT and entered service in October 1918, arriving in France only after the Armistice had been signed. In the interwar years, the US Army was reluctant to adopt the tank, assigning them to the role of infantry support, while the Cavalry developed the inadequate M1 Combat Car and M2 Light Tank. It was not until July 1940 that the Armor Branch of the US Army was formally created and late in 1941 that a tank – the M3 Lee Medium Tank – entered service that was a match for those of the Axis Powers. Some 6,200 were produced up to 1942 and they saw action in North Africa, on the Eastern Front and in the Pacific with the Americans and their allies.

From these inauspicious beginnings, however, the United States would soon emerge as one of the most important countries both for the production of tanks and the development of armoured warfare. The outbreak of war in December 1941 mobilised America's industrial might to produce weaponry on a hitherto unimagined scale. In February 1942 production began of the M4 Sherman, one of the most iconic tanks of all time. The Sherman tank, of which some 49,200 were built between 1942 and the end of the War, was one of the most important weapons of W II, serving in all theatres of war served as a potent symbol of A military and industrial power. While it may have been inferior to the German Panzer IV, Panther and Tiger tanks, the sheer number of Sherman tanks in the American and Allied armies prevailed. The M4 was gradually improved during the war, being fitted with the high-velocity M1 76mm gun. Other developments included the so-called 'wet' stowage of ammunition, designed to combat the Sherman's unenviable reputation for catching fire when hit, and improved suspension. The experience of the M4 Sherman against the heavier German tanks, however, showed the need for a heavier and more powerful tank.

This led to the development of the M26 Pershing. Armed with an M3 90mm gun it was the only US tank that could engage the German Panzer V Panther or Panzer VI Tiger and King Tiger on anything like equal terms. Eventually 2,222 were produced, but only twenty were delivered and saw action in Europe before the end of World War II. The Pershing was designed as a heavy tank, but in May 1946 it was redesignated as a medium tank. The M26 went on to serve with distinction during the Korean War, alongside the older M4A3E8 Sherman, proving itself far superior to the Chinese T-34/85, although its high fuel consumption and lack of mobility was somewhat exposed in the mountainous terrain of the Korean Peninsula.

M26 Pershings and M4A3E8 Shermans of the 73rd Heavy Tank Battalion at the Pusan Docks during the Korean War. (US National Archives)

THE DEVELOPMENT OF THE PATTON TANK

The design of the M26 Pershing set the pattern for American tanks until almost the end of the Cold War. This included torsion bar suspension, a low-profile design, a welded and cast hull, and turret made from a single steel casting. The M3 90mm gun also became the standard for US tanks of the early Cold War period. This coincided with an important shift in American attitudes towards the tank. World War II had confirmed the tank's place as a decisive weapon of war and in the months following the end of hostilities this was recognised both by the US military and industry. Tanks needed dedicated research, design, and development programmes and in April 1946 an industry committee, led by K.T. Keller of Chrysler, concluded that 'technological developments will continue to be the dominant factors in determining the outcome of wars between nations.' Thus, the continued development of the US tank force became one of the most important factors in the technological and industrial battle between America and the Soviet Union. In December 1950 a new Army Equipment Development Guide appeared stating that the mission of armour was 'the destruction of enemy forces by means of armor-protected firepower, mobility and shock action.' It recognised that the tank was the 'principal weapon of armor', committing the US military to an ongoing programme of tank development to ensure continued battlefield superiority over the Soviet Union.

Early experiences in World War II had already exposed the shortcomings of the M26. Fitted with the same engine as the M4A3 Sherman, it was woefully underpowered and work began in January

(below) A battle worn M46 among the mountainous terrain of Korea. The 90mm main gun proved superior to the 85mm gun of the Chinese T-34s, while its armour was more than adequate to counter the threats faced. (US National Archives)

1948 to fit a Continental AV1790-3 engine and Allison CD-850-1 transmission. The resulting M26E2 was considered a completely new tank and received the designation M46 in July that year, as well as being named after General George S. Patton Jr, the famous World War II commander and one of the pioneers of US armoured warfare. The Detroit Tank Plant set about converting existing M26s to M46 standard and manufacturing new tanks, but the plant's capacity had been run down after the end of World War II and when the Korean War broke out in 1950 the US military found itself short of tanks.

Production of the M46 began in November 1948 and the first tank arrived in Korea in August 1950. By the end of the year 200 M46s had been shipped to the peninsula, compared to 679 Shermans, 309 M26 Pershings and 138 M24 Chaffee light tanks. Throughout 1951 further M46s arrived in theatre, leading to the withdrawal of both the Pershing and Sherman from frontline units. In all, 1,160 M46 Pattons were built.

The M46 was always considered an interim measure and in December 1948 development had begun on a new tank, the T42. The specifications for the new 36-ton tank included better armour protection than the M46, a gun stabilised in both elevation and azimuth, and provision for an automatic loading system and stereoscopic range finder. In fact, the T42 was also underpowered with only the 500hp AOS-895 engine and the project was abandoned, but in September 1950 it was decided to fit the T42 turret to the M46 hull. The M46's Continental AV-1790-5B engine delivered 810hp and changes to the frontal armour significantly improved the new tank's survivability. It also featured a hull-mounted .30cal machine gun, the last American tank to do so. In December the tank received the designation M47. Testing of the prototypes led to the abandonment of the requirement for stabilisation of the main gun and the autoloader and in April

An M47 Patton on exercise in the United States in the 1950s. The hull machine gun, the last occasion on which this fitted to a US tank, is clearly evident. (Private collection)

1952 the tank was standardised as the M47 Patton. Production continued until November 1953, by which time 8,576 M47 Pattons had been built at the American Locomotive Company and in Detroit.

The M47 saw service with the US Army and the United States Marine Corps, as well as the National Guard. It was also exported to NATO countries, which adopted it as their standard Main Battle Tank alongside the British Centurion. Although it was withdrawn from US service from 1955 and declared obsolete two years later, it served widely with other nations. It saw action in the Indo-Pakistani wars of 1965 and 1971,

in the Iran-Iraq War and in various other conflicts from Africa to the Balkans.

Even before the M47 entered service, development was underway on a completely new tank. In October 1950 the decision was made to replace the M46 and M47. A newly designed elliptical hull and turret were required with a much larger turret ring, wider tracks, and the T139 90mm high-velocity main gun. The crew would be reduced from five to four by eliminating the hull-mounted machine gun. The new tank would be powered by the same Continental AV-1790-5B engine as the M47 and it would have a combat weight of 45

The T48 was the prototype for the M48 Patton. Note the characteristic elliptical turret and boat-like hull. (US National Archives)

The M48 proved its worth during the Vietnam War. Here an M48A3 of 1-69 Armor, 25th Infantry Division, moves through a destroyed Viet Cong camp as part of Operation Lincoln in 1966. (US National Archives)

tons. The perilous international situation of the early Cold War meant that the tank was rushed into production before proper testing. Chrysler was given an order for six prototypes and 542 production vehicles in December 1950 and in April 1953 the T48 was standardised as the M48 Patton. Almost 12,000 M48s were built between 1952 and 1959, making it one of the most important tanks of the Cold War period.

The M48 saw many developments and variations during its production history. Initially there were two variants in the production: the M48 had a Chrysler-designed cupola where the commander had to expose himself to fire the .50cal M2HB machine gun, while the M48A1 had a fully enclosed Aircraft Armament-designed cupola. The tank was also manufactured with both the Continental AV-1790-5B engine (Mod A) and, by American Locomotive, with the Continental AV-1790-5C engine (Mod B). The early M48s were also manufactured with different sized turret hatches for the commander and loader. The early M48s were plagued with teething problems because of being rushed into production. The engine suffered from excessive oil consumption and the range was limited to just 75 miles, insufficient for service in Europe. The new M12/T41 optical range finder also proved too fragile for the rigours of the field and early production M48s were restricted to service in the Continental United States. Nevertheless, between April 1952 and December 1954 some 7,000 M48 and M48A1 were produced.

In 1953 a major project began to increase the range and effectiveness of the M48 by fitting the more compact, fuel-injected AVI-1790-6 engine. Other changes included a simplified, more robust suspension and a new Cadillac Gage constant-pressure hydraulic gun elevation and control system. In December 1955 this entered production as the M48A2. With planned increases in tank production in the mid 1950s contracts for the M48A2 were awarded to Chrysler factory in Delaware, American Locomotive in New York, and General Motors in Grand Blanc, Michigan, although by the end of 1956 only the Chrysler factory was producing the M48A2. Further modifications were introduced including a M17 coincidence range finder, improved M5A2 ballistic drive and M13A3 gun data computer in the M13 Fire Control System resulting in the M48A2C. 1,344 of the previously produced 2,328 M4A2s were upgraded to C standard.

In June 1955 it was decided to adopt a diesel engine to deal with the perennial problems of range and fuel consumption that had dogged the M46/47 and M48 tanks. In August 1956 the AVDS-1790 diesel engine was adopted and the Army requested that around 1,020 M48A1 and M48A2 be fitted with the new power pack. By February the following year some 600 converted M48A3, as the diesel-powered version was known, were in service with the US Army and 419 with the US Marine Corps. As many M48A3s were converted from older models there was a great variation in their appearance, with some having older suspension, both early and light headlight configurations, and M48 and M48A1-style commander's cupolas. Chrysler produced new M48A3s alongside the conversion programme. Various detail improvements were introduced, as was a new commander's cupola, the M1E1.

The M48 proved itself an effective weapon of war in US service, albeit not in the role it was designed for. The M48 was withdrawn from US units in Germany in 1961 and replaced by the M60, but over 600 M48 Pattons served with both the Army and the Marine Corps in the Vietnam War between 1965 and 1973 where it operated mostly in an infantry support role.

The next stage of development was of crucial importance in the story of the Patton tank. In 1950 the Army had recommended the installation of a 105mm main gun, one of the reasons for the larger turret ring on the M48, and in July the following year trials were made to install just such a weapon with an automatic loader. The need for a more powerful main gun was made more urgent when a Soviet T-54 drove into the grounds of the British Embassy during the Hungarian Revolution of 1956. Initial examination of its armour and its 100mm main gun proved a bit of a wake-up call for US and British tank developers. The US Army began development of the XM60 – which would lead in time to the M60 – but the decision was taken not to install the T254 105mm gun in the M48 as sufficient numbers were not available, while the US Army had a large stockpile of 90mm ammunition. In fact, it was not until the mid 1970s that the remaining M48A3s, then still in service with the Army National

Guard, began to be fitted with the M68 105mm gun and new Fire Control System to be standardised as the M48A5. In all, 2,069 M48A3 were upgraded to A5 standard between October 1975 and December 1979.

The search for a successor to the M48 had been underway since the early 1950s. The prototype T95 medium, featuring innovative siliceous-cored armour and the T208 90mm smoothbore gun, was rejected in favour of a cheaper, more fuel-efficient tank. In September 1957 plans were tabled for a new tank armed with a 105mm gun and with a redesigned hull. In 1958 competitive testing of 90mm and 120mm guns, alongside the British L7 105mm and American T254E1 took place at the Aberdeen Proving Grounds. The British gun came out on top, although for various reasons the T254 was chosen for the new production tank.

That year four versions of the XM60 were submitted for evaluation. The first had the 120mm gun in the T95E6 elongated turret; the second had the 105mm T254E2 rifled gun in the T95E5 turret and M48A2-style cupola; the third mounted the 90mm gun in the T95E6 turret; while the final one had the T95E1 turret and a 90mm gun. The hulls used were modified M48A2 hulls with three return rollers, six roadwheels and no shock absorbers. In August 1958 the T254E2 was accepted as the main gun of the new tank and standardised as the M68. In December 1958 the XM60 was ordered into production and in March the following year the tank was officially renamed the M60.

The M48A5 was the final development of the Patton series of medium tanks, fitting an M68 105mm gun to the M48A3. In this configuration the M48 continued to serve in Army National Guard Units into the 1980s. (US Army photo by Sgt. Marvin D. Lynchard)

THE M60

The Tank, Combat, Full Tracked: 105mm Gun, M60 that was standardised in March 1959 was both a continuation of the Patton family of medium tanks and a new chapter in the history of US tank development. In 1957, as a result of a congressional enquiry, the Department of Defense had established the Armament for Future Tanks or Similar Combat Vehicles (ARCOVE) group. The group suggested the phasing out of the current establishment of light, medium and heavy tanks in favour of a new Main Battle Tank (MBT) equipped to survive the envisaged nuclear battlefield of any future war with the Soviet Union. This would be complemented by a light amphibious and air-portable AFV similar to the Soviet PT-76. The new MBT would be based on the T95 prototype and incorporate innovative armour technology. As we have seen, the T95 programme foundered and in 1958 it was replaced by the XM60 that would become, a year later, the M60. The M60 was to incorporate the 105mm M68 gun in an elongated turret similar to that used on the T95, but these would not be ready in time so the first M60s were manufactured with the M68 installed in the turret of the M48A2. In the same month as the M60 was standardised, the Tank Automotive and Armaments Command (TACOM) recommended the development of a new MBT armed with a 152mm missile-firing main gun and an aluminium-hulled armoured reconnaissance/airborne assault amphibious AFV to replace the M41 Walker Bulldog light tank, the M60 and the M103 heavy tank.

The M60 – which never officially received the name Patton – was thus at once both an interim solution born out of the expediency that had characterised the US tank programme since 1945 and a new beginning, being the first American MBT. Production of an initial batch of 180 vehicles was ordered in June 1959 and between July and October that year four tanks were made by Chrysler and handed over to the US Army for testing. These initial tests revealed problems with the suspension caused by the lack of shock absorbers, but as full production was already underway the first tanks to leave the production line at Chrysler's factory in Newark, Delaware, were not fitted with the recommended additional shock absorbers. 360 tanks were made at Newark before production shifted to the Detroit Tank Arsenal in 1960 and when production ceased in October 1962 2,205 M60s had been manufactured.

THE M60 DESCRIBED

The first M60s – or 'Slick Sixty' as they became known – looked very similar to the M48 and quite distinct from subsequent versions of the M60. The main distinguishing feature between the new tanks and its predecessor was the replacement of the M48's boat-shaped hull with a new wedge-shaped front designed to allow the easy adoption of new armour technology. The tank was 9.309m long (with the gun tube pointing forward), 3.362m wide and 3.206m high. The weight was 45 tons. Angled at between 55° and 63°, the frontal hull armour varied in thickness from 93mm to 143mm. The side armour was between 36mm and 74mm, while the hull roof armour was 36mm and the floor 19mm at the front, decreasing to

An M60 at the Fort Lewis Military Museum, MI. Note the bore evacuator on the main gun tube, designed to prevent harmful gasses being released into the turret, the M19 Commander's Cupola, and the elliptical turret of the M48. (Articseahorse)

(right) A line up of 'Slick Sixties' in Germany in the early 1960s. Note all have the M85 HMG fitted and the AN/VSS-1 searchlight. (US Army)

13mm at the rear. The hull held 26 rounds of 105mm ammunition in two racks either side of the driver's compartment. The driver's and fighting compartment were served by a gas particulate filter system which fed purified air in the event of NBC contamination and served as a heater for the crew compartment.

The M60 was powered by a Continental AVDS-1790-2 V-12 diesel engine delivering 750hp. The Allison CD-850-6 transmission provided two forward gears and one reverse. On the first M60s the tank was steered by a wheel, which was later replaced by a T-shaped steering column. The suspension consisted of torsion bars, a front idler wheel and six road wheels, and a rear drive sprocket. From 1962 the hydraulic shock absorbers were fitted on the first and last road wheel stations and two bumper springs (two at the front and one at the rear). The roadwheels were smaller than those of the M48A2 and constructed from aluminium with only a steel ring included for strength in an attempt to keep the tank's weight down. The tank was fitted with T97 double-pin tracks, eighty links each side, with chevron-patterned rubber pads.

The original turret fitted to the M60 was that of the M48A2. It was a one-piece steel casting with frontal armour between 85mm and 143mm thick. On the sides the armour thickness ranged from 36mm to 74mm, while on the roof it was 36mm. The M116 gun mount, with 114mm of armour, housed the M68 105mm gun and a coaxial 7.62mm machine gun. The commander enjoyed a M19 Commander's Cupola with all-round vision provided by eight vision blocks and an M28C Periscope Sight. The M19 was fitted with a .50cal M85 heavy machine gun, but on the early M60 turrets there was also a mount attached to the left-hand side of the M19 Commander's Cupola for a .50cal M2HB heavy machine gun as the M85 was not yet available in sufficient quantities. The M68 gun had available M392 and M392A2 Armour-Piercing Discarding Sabot with Tracer (APDS-T), M393 and M393A1 High Explosive Plastic with Tracer (HEP-T), and T384 High Explosive Anti-Tank with Tracer (HEAT-T) rounds. In addition to the 26 rounds stored in the hull, there were nine stored in a rack on floor of the turret basket, sixteen at the loader's station, and a further six in the turret bustle (increased to eight later when the smaller AN/VRC radio was installed). There were also 5,950 rounds of 7.62mm ammunition and 420 rounds of .50cal ammunition.

The primary Fire Control System (FCS) included an M17C Rangefinder, M13A1D analogue Ballistics Computer, M10 Ballistic Drive, M31 Periscope, and power unit. This system was virtually unchanged from the M48A2C. A secondary FCS consisted of a M105C Telescope. The M60 was also fitted with the AN/VSS-1 2.2kw Xenon searchlight. This could provide both infra-red and visible light and was mounted just above the gun tube. It could be stored in a bracket on the rear left-hand side of the turret when not in use. Early M60s were fitted with the older Crouse-Hinds 18" Tank Searchlight Model 44676-C, standard on earlier Patton tanks, which could only provide white illumination.

The tank was initially fitted with AN/GRC radios and an AN/VIA-4 intercommunication system. The radio equipment was housed at the rear of the turret. The radio system allowed communication between crew members and with other tanks, as well as – via the External Interphone Control Box C-1633/VIA-4 – with accompanying infantry. The M60 used the AT-803/VR and AT-912/VRC antennas fitted at three stations on the turret roof.

Initial testing of the M60 was positive. The 105mm gun was well received and the increased combat range was a major improvement on the previous Patton tanks. The four prototypes and fifteen of the early production vehicles had insufficient armour thickness, to keep their weight down, and these were relegated to driver training duties at the US Army's Armor School at Fort Knox, Kentucky. The first M60s arrived in Germany at the end of 1960 but equipping of units with the new tanks was a slow process because of limited stocks of equipment, such as the M85 machine gun, and ammunition for the main gun. By the late 1960s the 'Slick Sixty' was being phased out of frontline units in favour of the M60A1, but it continued to serve with Army National Guard units well into the 1980s. As late as 1985 two battalions of Army National Guard equipped with M60s took part in Exercise Central Guardian, part of the annual REFORGER exercise in Germany.

An M60A1 of 1-77 Armor, 4th Infantry Division, in April 1974. It is difficult to tell from most photos precisely what version of the M60A1 is pictured but given the date this is most likely an M60A1 (AOS). (US National Archives)

M60A1

Although the M60 was initially fitted with the same turret as the M48A2, the development of a new turret based on that of the prototype T95 continued. Despite the lack of advanced siliceous cored armour, the elongated shape offered better ballistic protection for the crew and more space. The first prototypes with the new turret – the M60E1 – were completed in May and June 1961. The M60E1 also incorporated improvements suggested by the first tests of the M60. These included hydraulic shock absorbers on the first and last road wheel stations, a new arrangement for the accelerator and gear pedals, and a T-bar steering wheel. New seats were also installed for all the crew members, replacing the unpopular wire mesh seats in the M60, including two for the commander allowing him to stand in the open cupola.

The M60E1 also included a XM16C electric computer and new optics for both the gunner and commander. The gunner's XM35 periscope allowed both normal and infrared vision and was directly linked to the ballistic drive. The commander's M17C coincidence sight and rangefinder allowed a x10 magnification, while the M19 cupola had both the XM34 daylight periscope and a XM36 combination periscope for night vision. Initially the FCS was the same on production tanks as that on the M60, but these were replaced by the M17A1 rangefinder and the M13A2 Ballistic Computer.

On 22 October 1961 the new tank was standardised as the M60A1. It was classified as Standard A, with the M60 being Standard B. Production of the latter tank ceased

An M60A1 of 3-64 Armor, 3rd Infantry Division. It wears the experimental MASSTER camouflage scheme developed by the US Seventh Army in Germany in the early 1970s. (Hans Stenzel via Carl Schulze)

Another M60A1 sporting the MASSTER camouflage scheme drives through a German town during the autumn of 1975. Note the placement of the heavy cable connecting the AN/VSS-1 searchlight. (US National Archives)

and that of the first order of 720 M60A1 began immediately. Production M60A1 also had their frontal armour increased from a minimum of 93mm to 104mm, while the turret armour was also improved giving it the same protection as the M103 heavy tank. Other production changes included the introduction of a new Continental AVDS-1790-2A engine, which was slightly heavier but gave improved fuel efficiency.

The M60A1 saw the weight increase to 47 tons necessitating shock absorbers on the front two and last road wheels, instead of the just the first and last stations on the M60E1. The coaxial M73 machine gun was also later replaced by the M219. The M68 gun was also replaced by the M68E1 which featured better hydraulics and stabilisation. The first M60A1 were delivered to units in Germany in the spring of 1962.

An M88A1 Armored Recovery Vehicle tows an M60A1 in the lead up to Exercise Certain Shield, the field exercise component of REFORGER 78. (US Army photo by Keith A Dixon)

M60A1 (AOS)

Despite being originally developed as an interim solution to the United States' need to develop tanks capable of facing the latest generation of Soviet machines, by the late 1960s it was clear that the M60 would provide the bulk of the US Army's armour well into the next decade. The much-vaunted MBT70 project, developed jointly by the USA and West Germany, was floundering and was eventually abandoned in 1971. Development of the M60 continued

alongside the MBT70 project in the late 'sixties and included proposals for a new high-velocity 120mm gun and a tube-over-bar suspension system. While these projects had some merits, developments stalled as the Army's resources were directed into the Vietnam War. In January 1970, however, the Chief of Staff approved a comprehensive programme of product improvements to the M60. Beginning the following year, a new top loading air cleaner (TLAC) was fitted which prolonged engine life by reducing the amount of dirt and dust drawn into the engine. In 1972 new production tanks were fitted with Add-On Stablization (AOS) designed to fit onto the existing gun hydraulic system and improve accuracy when firing on the move. The stabilisers had been developed in the mid-1960s and were already in use on the West German Leopard 1. They increased the probability of hitting a target when on the move to some fifty percent. The M60 was also fitted with a new T142 steel track. This double-pin track was a significant improvement over the existing T97 and had removable octagonal rubber pads. Tanks with the new tracks, gun stabilisation system, and new air cleaners were subsequently known as Tank, Combat, Full Tracked: 105mm Gun M60A1 (AOS).

(left) An M60A1 (AOS) of 3-63 Armor. Note the unusual stowage fitted to the cage at the rear of the turret and the typically large amount of gear carried. (Hans Stenzel via Carl Schulze)

(below) An M60A1 (AOS) of 11th Armored Cavalry Regiment photographed in September 1974 has the Top-Loading Air Cleaners but is still fitted with the T97 tracks. (Hans Stenzel via Carl Schulze)

An atmospheric shot of an M60A1 of 3rd Cavalry Regiment taken in January 1977. This image shows the T142 tracks with their detachable rubber pads. (US National Archives)

M60A1 (RISE)

The early seventies were a crucial time for US tank development. The abandonment of the MBT70 programme, the increasing drain on resources on resources caused by the war in Vietnam, and the Détente policy of Richard Nixon and Henry Kissinger towards the Soviet Union all contributed to a declining interest in and production of main battle tanks in America. However, in October 1973 Syria and Egypt and their Arab allies launched a surprise attack on the US's ally Israel. Between the outbreak of the Yom Kippur War and the end of the year the US delivered large amounts of military equipment, including 200 M60 and M48 tanks to Israel. The M60 had first been sold to Israel in the wake of the 1967 Six-Day War and proved itself a rugged and capable weapon. This emergency delivery of tanks to Israel came mainly from US Army reserve stocks and revealed that the US lacked the manufacturing capacity to meet the demands for new tanks if the international situation worsened. When new tank production was only some forty a month, suddenly the military demanded several hundred new tanks. In December 1974 Major General Chester McKeen was appointed the 'Czar for Tanks', resulting in a more centralised system of tank production in dedicated tank factories and of tank development.

The 'tank crisis' of 1973 led two years later to the next stage in the M60's development, the M60A1 (RISE). The Reliability Improved Selected Equipment (RISE) programme saw the installation of a new Continental AVDS-1790-2C engine with stronger cylinders, a modified fuel system, and improved starter leading to increased reliability and service life. During the RISE improvements between 1975 and 1977 the engine also received a new oil-cooled alternator, solid-state regulator, and a wiring harness with quick disconnects.

1973 was also an important in the history of the M60 as in that year the three regular US Marine Corps tank battalions retired the last of their M103A2 heavy tanks and M48A3 Pattons. The M60 had not seen service with either the US Army or Marine Corps in Vietnam, but with its introduction to the USMC it became established as the principal main battle tank of the US military with the M48 being relegated to Army National Guard units. In all, before production ceased of the M60A1 in 1980, a total of 578 were delivered to the USMC where they served with the three regular tank battalions (1st, 2nd and 3rd based at Camp Pendleton and Twenty-Nine Palms in Florida and Camp Lejeune in North Carolina respectively) and the two reserve battalions, the 4th and 8th.

An M60A1 (RISE Passive) wearing wearing a non-standard MERDC camouflage scheme during REFORGER 1977. (US Army photo by Spc5 Danny P. Finlay)

A rather battered looking M60A1 at the US Armor School at Fort Knox, KY, in 1984. (US Army photo by Eddie McCrossan)

M60A1 (RISE Passive)

From May 1972 work was underway to develop a further improved version of the M60. By March the following year twelve prototypes had been built under the designation M60A1E3. They included all the features of the M60A1 (AOS) and (RISE) but they were also fitted with a laser range finder, solid-state computer, and the experimental tube-over-bar suspension. The tanks were also fitted with a new AN/VSS-3A searchlight. This was smaller than the AN/VSS-1 searchlight and produced both white and infrared light. Both the gunner and tank commander received passive night sights, while the barrel of the M68 105mm was enclosed in a thermal shield designed to solve the issue of distortion resulting from uneven heating or cooling of the gun tube. These changes and a few others would go on, as we shall see, to be standardised as the M60A3, but from 1977 many of the improvements were included in the production of M60A1s. These included the passive periscope sights for the gunner and commander, an AN/VVS-2(V)1 night vision device for the driver, and a new deep-water fording kit. In 1978 M239 smoke grenade launchers were fitted to either side of the turret and a new 7.62mm M240 machine gun installed as the co-axial weapon, as well as a Vehicle Engine Exhaust Smoke System (VEESS) to offer a simple smoke screen capacity. Kevlar spall liners were also installed in the turret. Finally, the tank was upgraded with an improved AVDS-1790-2D engine. With these changes the tank was designated Tank, Combat, Full-Tracked: 105mm M60A1 (RISE Passive).

The M60A1 (RISE Passive) also had the capability to mount Explosive Reactive Armour (ERA) plates on the turret and glacis plate. Concerns over the M60A1's ability to defend against the widespread adoption of anti-tank guided missiles (ATGM), such as the 9M14 Malyutka (or AT-3 'Sagger' to use its NATO reporting name), by America's potential enemies had increased during the early 1970s. The use of ERA had been tested and perfected by the Israel Defense Forces and was first used in battle on their M60A1s and Centurion tanks during the 1982 war in Lebanon. The survivability of the M60A1 became an increasing concern for the USMC during the 1980s. The resulting upgrade for the M60A1 consisted of different-sized panels of ERA, each made up of a plastic explosive charge sandwiched between steel plates. These were mounted on frames designed to detonate the ERA panels at a prescribed distance from the hull or turret armour. ERA was effective against High-Explosive Anti-Tank (HEAT) rounds, ATGMs and infantry weapons like the RPG-7, as well as against kinetic energy rounds fired by other MBTs. The weight penalty for this additional protection was minimal and the principal drawback was any ERA panel could only resist a single hit, while its detonation was a hazard to accompanying infantry. A very similar system was developed by the US Army in the 1980s for the M60A3, although it did not enter general service as the M1 Abrams was equipped with Chobham-type armour and was expected to replace the M60A3 by the early 1990s. The ERA system was tested on the Army's M60A3 and even though several vehicles were converted for

An M60A1 (RISE Passive) of 1st Tank Battalion, USMC, during Exercise Solid Shield in May 1983. (USMC photo by LCpl. C.C. Jackson)

Another M60A1 (RISE Passive) of 1st Tank Battalion during Exercise Kernel Potlatch in 1986. Note the deep wading tube fitted to the rear and the smaller AN/VSS-3A searchlight. (USMC photo by PH2 Paul Pappas)

National Guard use, most of the production kits were procured by the USMC for their M60A1 (RISE Passive).

Between October 1962 and May 1980, a total of 7,948 M60A1s left the production line. Of these 578 were delivered to the USMC from 1973, while 874 went to foreign users, including Ethiopia, Israel, Iran, Italy and Sudan. Other M60A1s were delivered to foreign powers from the early 1980s as the tank was upgraded to M60A3 standard or replaced by the M1 Abrams in the US Army. The USMC began to take delivery of the new M1A1 Abrams from the late 1980s but maintained the M60A1 (RISE Passive) in service until 1991 and it served with distinction during the first Gulf War.

A USMC M60A1 (RISE Passive) fitted with ERA panels during Exercise Solid Shield 1989. (USMC photo by SSgt. Scott Stewart)

M60A2

The ARCOVE report of January 1958 had recommended that American tank development concentrate on two vehicles: a main battle tank and an Armored Reconnaissance/Airborne Assault Vehicle (AR/AAV). Both would be fitted with a main weapon capable of firing guided missiles, the weapon system which, the authors considered, would dominate the battlefield of the second half of the twentieth century. In June the following year the Aeronautics Division of the Ford Motor Company began development of the XM13 Shillelagh Combat Vehicle Weapons System. This was to be fired from the XM81 152mm gun-launcher, which would also be capable of firing conventional munitions. At half the weight and length of the M68 105mm gun, the XM81 was an enticing prospect for tank designers. The XM81's conventional rounds – HEAT, white phosphorous and a training round – would be spin stabilised by the rifling on the 152mm tube, but also featured a unique combustible-case design. The XM81 was the central feature of both the new M551 Sheridan AR/AAV and the proposed MBT70.

The first successful launch of the Shillelagh missile took place in September 1961 and in August 1964 the missile was approved for low-rate production. The Army were determined to press ahead with the project, despite its obvious shortcomings and the technical problems that had dogged the projects since its inception. Just three months later it entered serial production.

Despite the problems with the XM81, efforts had been underway since 1961 to develop

(above) The prototype M60A1E2 fitted with the Type B turret. (US Army photo courtesy of the Patton Museum)

(below) M60A2s of 1-67 Armor take part in field exercises at Fort Hood, TX, in April 1975. These are early production vehicles, identifiable by the bore evacuator on the 152mm gun-launcher and the T97 chevron tracks. (US National Archives)

the new gun-launcher for use in the M60 tank. An M60 tank chassis was fitted with a dummy turret to house the gun-launcher and designated M60E2. Subsequently, three T95 turrets and two modified M60E1 turrets were fitted with the XM81 and mated to the M48 hull for further testing. In January

....text continued on page 45

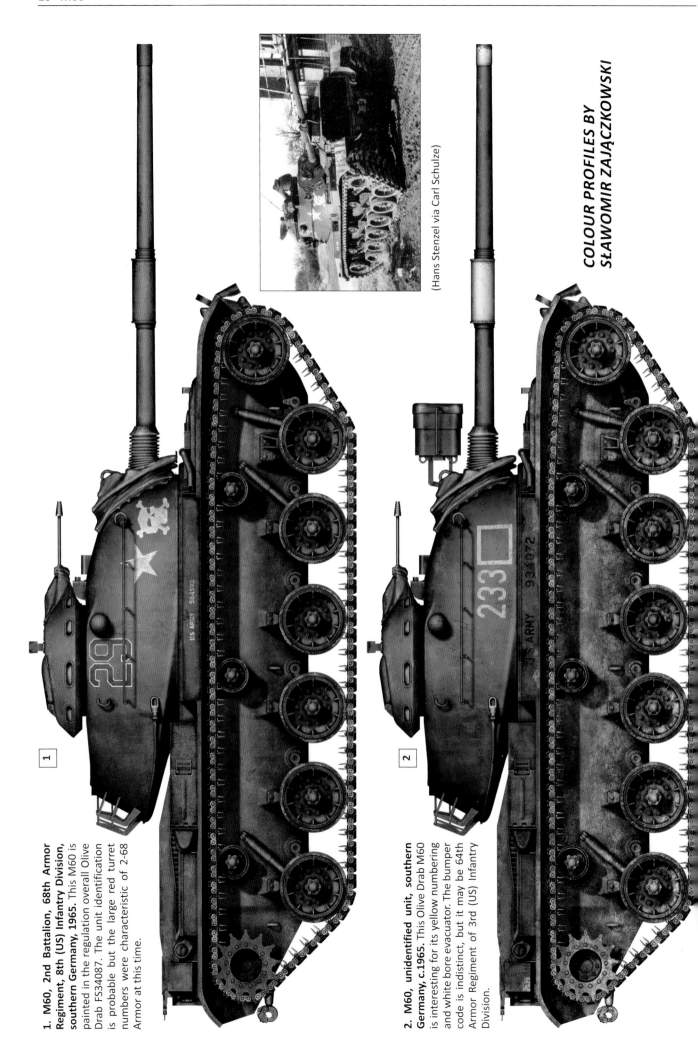

COLOUR PROFILES BY SŁAWOMIR ZAJĄCZKOWSKI

1

1. M60, 2nd Battalion, 68th Armor Regiment, 8th (US) Infantry Division, southern Germany, 1965. This M60 is painted in the regulation overall Olive Drab FS34087. The unit identification is probable but the large red turret numbers were characteristic of 2-68 Armor at this time.

2

2. M60, unidentified unit, southern Germany, c.1965. This Olive Drab M60 is interesting for its yellow numbering and white bore evacuator. The bumper code is indistinct, but it may be 64th Armor Regiment of 3rd (US) Infantry Division.

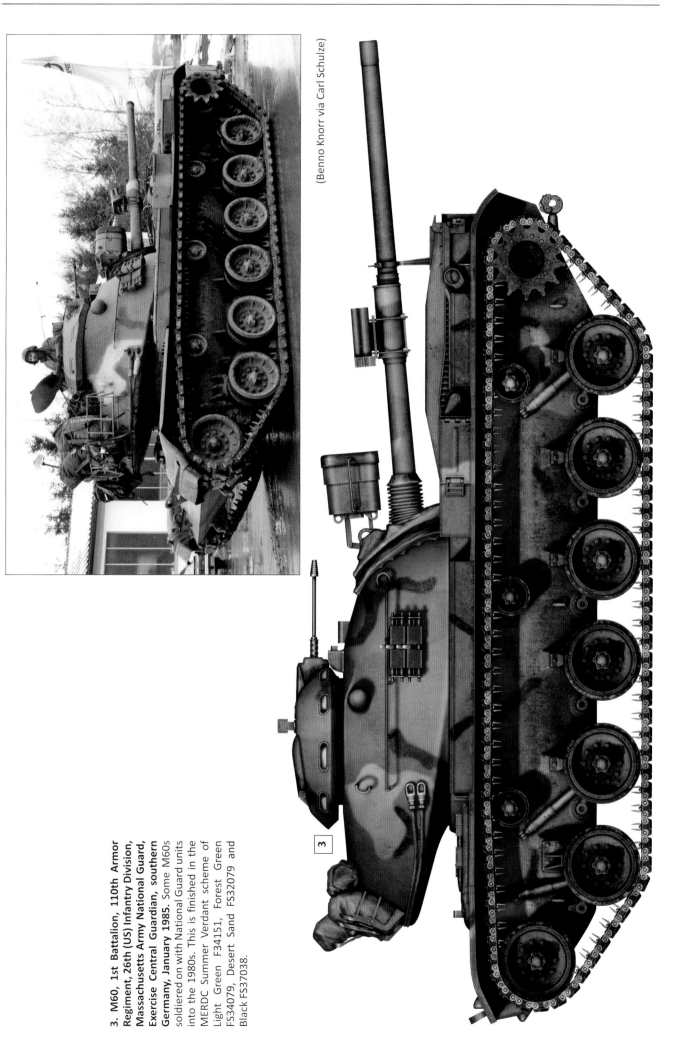

(Benno Knorr via Carl Schulze)

3. **M60, 1st Battalion, 110th Armor Regiment, 26th (US) Infantry Division, Massachusetts Army National Guard, Exercise Central Guardian, southern Germany, January 1985.** Some M60s soldiered on with National Guard units into the 1980s. This is finished in the MERDC Summer Verdant scheme of Light Green F34151, Forest Green FS34079, Desert Sand FS32079 and Black FS37038.

3

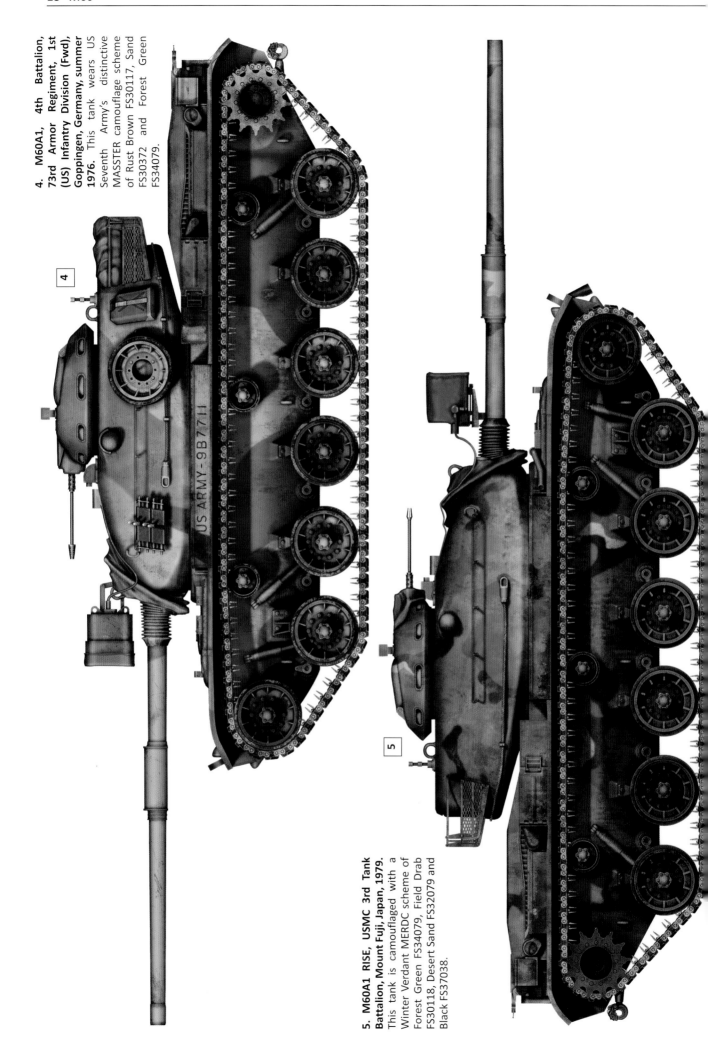

4. M60A1, 4th Battalion, 73rd Armor Regiment, 1st (US) Infantry Division (Fwd), Goppingen, Germany, summer 1976. This tank wears US Seventh Army's distinctive MASSTER camouflage scheme of Rust Brown FS30117, Sand FS30372 and Forest Green FS34079.

5. M60A1 RISE, USMC 3rd Tank Battalion, Mount Fuji, Japan, 1979. This tank is camouflaged with a Winter Verdant MERDC scheme of Forest Green FS34079, Field Drab FS30118, Desert Sand FS32079 and Black FS37038.

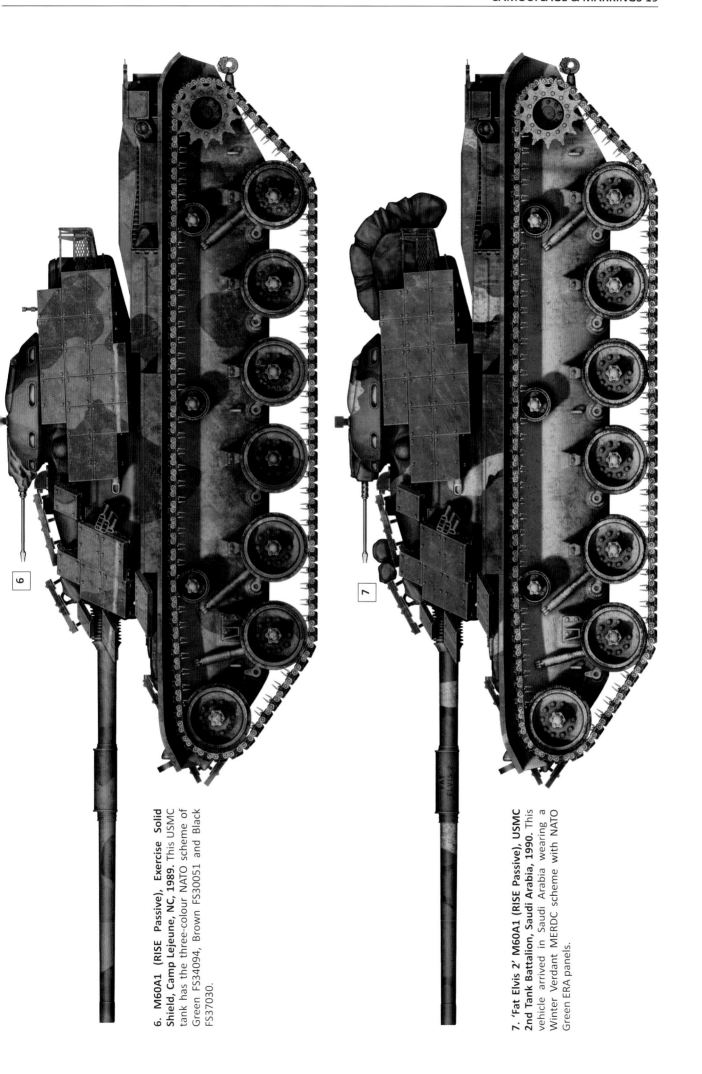

6. **M60A1 (RISE Passive), Exercise Solid Shield, Camp Lejeune, NC, 1989.** This USMC tank has the three-colour NATO scheme of Green FS34094, Brown FS30051 and Black FS37030.

7. **'Fat Elvis 2' M60A1 (RISE Passive), USMC 2nd Tank Battalion, Saudi Arabia, 1990.** This vehicle arrived in Saudi Arabia wearing a Winter Verdant MERDC scheme with NATO Green ERA panels.

8. M60A1 (RISE Passive), USMC 2nd Tank Battalion, Saudi Arabia, January 1991. This tank, fitted with an M9 dozer blade, is painted with an overall coat of Desert Tan FS33446.

(USMC photo by Staff Sgt. M.D. Masters)

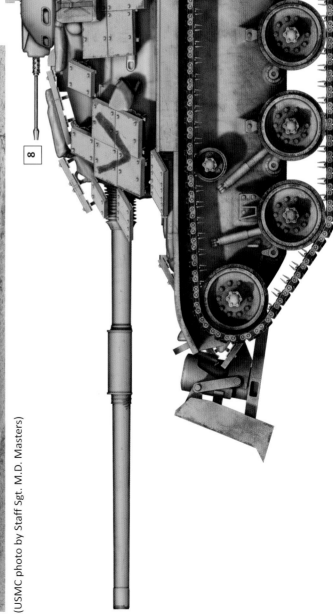

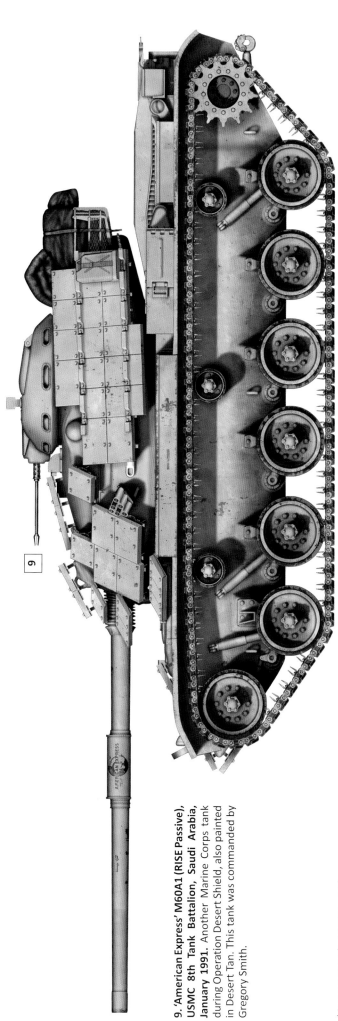

9. 'American Express' M60A1 (RISE Passive), USMC 8th Tank Battalion, Saudi Arabia, January 1991. Another Marine Corps tank during Operation Desert Shield, also painted in Desert Tan. This tank was commanded by Gregory Smith.

(Gregory Smith, USMC retd.)

(Gregory Smith, USMC retd.)

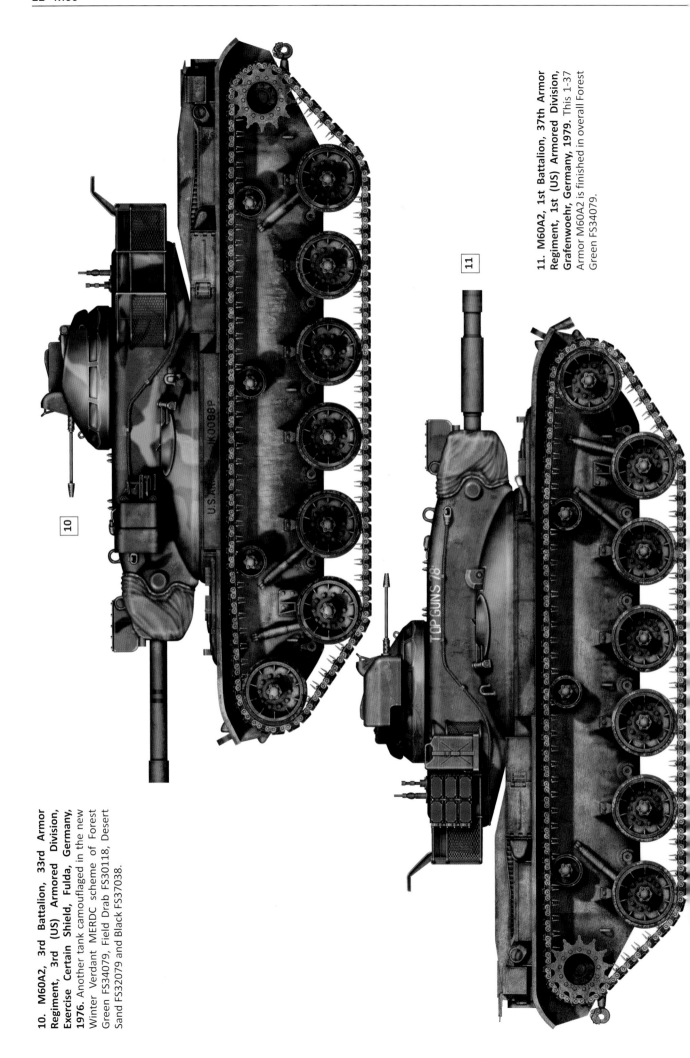

10. M60A2, 3rd Battalion, 33rd Armor Regiment, 3rd (US) Armored Division, Exercise Certain Shield, Fulda, Germany, 1976. Another tank camouflaged in the new Winter Verdant MERDC scheme of Forest Green FS34079, Field Drab FS30118, Desert Sand FS32079 and Black FS37038.

11. M60A2, 1st Battalion, 37th Armor Regiment, 1st (US) Armored Division, Grafenwoehr, Germany, 1979. This 1-37 Armor M60A2 is finished in overall Forest Green FS34079.

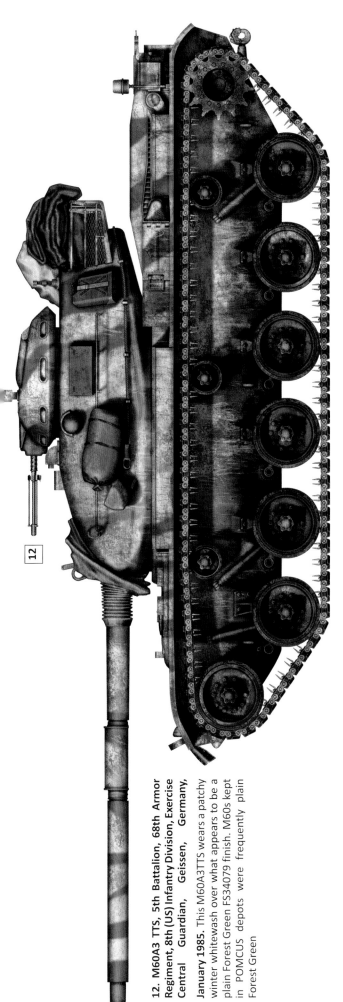

12

12. M60A3 TTS, 5th Battalion, 68th Armor Regiment, 8th (US) Infantry Division, Exercise Central Guardian, Geissen, Germany, January 1985. This M60A3TTS wears a patchy winter whitewash over what appears to be a plain Forest Green FS34079 finish. M60s kept in POMCUS depots were frequently plain Forest Green

US Army photo by Tech. Sgt. Boyd Belcher)

An 1-4 Infantry M60A3 TTS with the attachment for the M9 dozer blade fitted. (Chris Mrosko)

13. M60A3 TTS, 1st Battalion, 4th Infantry Regiment, Combat Maneuver Training Center, Hohenfels, Germany, 1990. This was the US Army unit to operate the M60 as OPFOR at the CMTR. It is finished in an overall camouflage of NATO Green FS34094.

13

M60A0

1ST BATTALION, 110TH ARMOR REGIMENT, 26TH (US) INFANTRY DIVISION, MASSACHUSETTS ARMY NATIONAL GUARD,

EXERCISE CENTRAL GUARDIAN, SOUTHERN GERMANY, JANUARY 1985.

1/35 SCALE
AFV CLUB, DEF MODEL, LEGEND PRODUCTIONS
UWE KERN

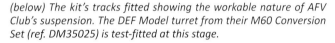

(below) There are some minor adjustments needed to backdate AFV Club's M60A3 hull to a 'Slick 60', notably moving the first return roller back by 5mm and omitting the second of the two front shock absorbers.

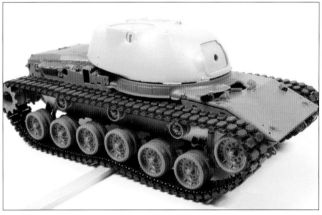

(below) The kit's tracks fitted showing the workable nature of AFV Club's suspension. The DEF Model turret from their M60 Conversion Set (ref. DM35025) is test-fitted at this stage.

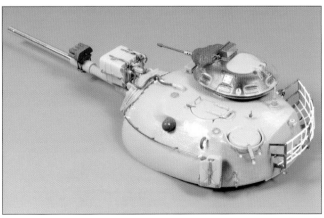

(above) DEF Model's turret assembled and detailed. The early-style rear stowage rack was made from plastic rod, while the side rails were made from copper wire for greater strength. Other details come from the DEF Model conversion set and the AFV Club kit.

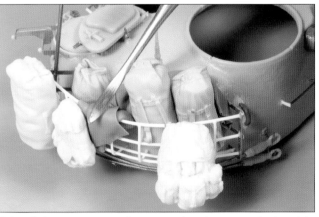

(above) The stowage came from Legend Productions and Sol Models. Green Stuff two-part epoxy putty was used to make some natural-looking tarpaulins.

(above) The distinctive Summer Verdant MERDC camouflage was carefully drawn in outline, then masked and airbrushed using Humbrol and Revell enamels.

(above) Echelon Fine Details offer a set of generic US Army bumper codes (ref. D356237), ideal for modelling specific vehicles like this one.

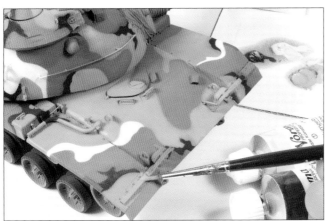

(above) The model was weathered principally with oil paints and pigments.

(above) The Legend Productions' M85 Cupola (ref. LF1249) is a superb little kit in its own right and has a nicely reproduced interior.

(below) Leopard Workshop's US-style AS-1729 Aerials on MX-6707 Base Unit (ref. LW021B) add a level of detail to any M60 kit.

(below) Valkyrie's Modern US Tank Crew (ref. 35017) are perfect for 1970s and early '80s REFORGER projects.

M60A1

1-11 ARMORED CAVALRY REGIMENT, 3RD ARMORED DIVISION, US SEVENTH ARMY, FULDA, GERMANY, SUMMER 1976.

1/35 SCALE
TAKOM
DAVID GRUMMITT

(below) Takom's M60 hull, suspension and running gear are very nicely detailed and probably the best available in 1/35 scale.

(right) Assembly is relatively quick once the suspension is complete and, as you can see, the fit is first-rate.

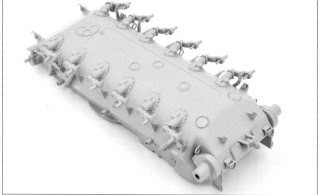

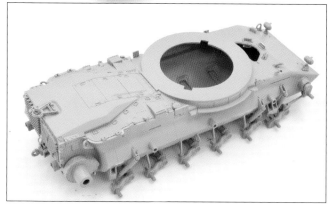

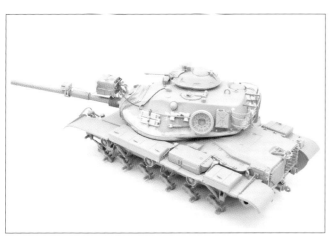

(above) The kit was built out of the box, apart from the Hoffman Device from the Tamiya accessories set (ref. 35141) and the resin stowage from the Legend Productions set (ref. L1316). The only addition was a cable to the AN/VSS-1 searchlight.

(above right) The outlines of the MASSTER camouflage were outlined with a brush using Vallejo acrylics before being filled in with the airbrush.

(right) The completed MASSTER camouflage is certainly very eye-catching.

(bottom) The MASSTER camouflage was applied in a variety of different patterns. Note the stowage typical of US 7th Army M60A1s during the 1970s. (Hans Stenzel via Carl Schulze)

M60A1 (RISE Passive)

3RD PLATOON, ALPHA COMPANY, 8TH TANK BATTALION, UNITED STATES MARINE CORPS, KUWAIT, FEBRUARY 1991.

1/35 SCALE
TAKOM
DAVID GRUMMITT

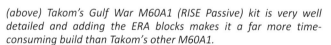

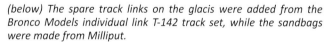

(above) Takom's Gulf War M60A1 (RISE Passive) kit is very well detailed and adding the ERA blocks makes it a far more time-consuming build than Takom's other M60A1.

(below) The spare track links on the glacis were added from the Bronco Models individual link T-142 track set, while the sandbags were made from Milliput.

(above) The 8th Tank Battalion's M60A1s are very well documented and the various stowage arrangements on individual tanks changed during the course of their deployment to Saudi Arabia and Kuwait during the First Gulf War.

(below) Vallejo's US Modern Desert Colors set (71.029) was used to paint the base colour. The set contains five different paints designed to offer a modulated finish.

Left) MIG Productions' Dark Wash was applied as a pin wash to pick out the details after the kit decals were applied. The tank name – 'Beirut Payback' – was a reference to the 1983 bombing of the USMC barracks in that city.

(below) The stowage was a mixture of Legend Productions and Tamiya items secured in place with thin strips of Tamiya masking tape.

(below) A line of LVTP-7s led by an USMC M60A1 (RISE Passive) fitted with a Pearson Mine Plow during Operation Desert Shield. (USMC photo by SSgt. Masters)

M60A2

1-35 ARMORED REGIMENT, 1ST ARMORED DIVISION, US SEVENTH ARMY, ERLANGEN, GERMANY, 1976.

1/35 SCALE AFV CLUB DAVID CHOU

(below) AFV Club produce two M60A2 kits, this one (ref. AF35230) and one with the early-style barrel with bore evacuator (ref. AF35238).

(below) The kit was built out of the box, except for the addition of some resin stowage.

The model was painted using Gunze Sangyo Mr Hobby acrylics and finished in the Summer Verdant MERDC scheme.

M60A3 TTS

1ST BATTALION, 4TH INFANTRY REGIMENT, COMBAT MANEUVER TRAINING CENTER, HOHENFELS, GERMANY, 1990.

1/72 SCALE
REVELL
DAVID GRUMMITT

(below) Blackdog's resin accessory set is designed for an Operation Desert Storm M60A1, including a complete and very busy rear stowage rack which simply attaches to the rear of the turret.

(above) Revell's M60 builds into a nice model out of the box but can be improved by the addition of Hauler's photoetch set, which includes such items as the fender supports.

(below) The beautifully moulded stowage from the Blackdog set repay some careful painting with Vallejo acrylics.

(above) Vallejo's Russian Green 4BO Surface Primer (74.609) is the perfect way to start painting the tank. Subsequent applications of Tamiya acrylics and the weathering will shift the appearance towards the characteristic dull green of 1-4 Infantry's OPFOR tanks.

M60A3 TTS
5TH BATTALION, 77TH ARMOR REGIMENT 'STEEL TIGERS', 8TH (US) INFANTRY DIVISION,

EXERCISE CERTAIN CHALLENGE, SOUTHERN GERMANY, SEPTEMBER 1988.
1/35 SCALE, ACADEMY, JOSÉ LUIS LOPEZ RUIZ

(below) The Academy M60A1 base kit was their IDF Blazer ERA version (ref. 1358). The lower hull and running gear were assembled largely out of the box (including the aluminium roadwheels) and some additional texture was added with Tamiya Plastic Putty.

(below) The Legend Productions' upgrade set (ref. LF1248) is designed to enhance both the old Tamiya and Academy kits. It contains a new gun mantlet and M68A1 barrel, a M19 commander's cupola and a host of other details.

(above) The refined detail of the resin parts is evident on the rear of the tank.

(above and centre) The assembled model ready for paint. Despite its age, the Academy kit builds up nicely and can easily be bought up to an acceptable level with some small additions.

(left) This model really shows the importance of assembling, placing, painting and weathering a good array of stowage to make a convincing replica of an M60.k.

M728 COMBAT ENGINEER VEHICLE

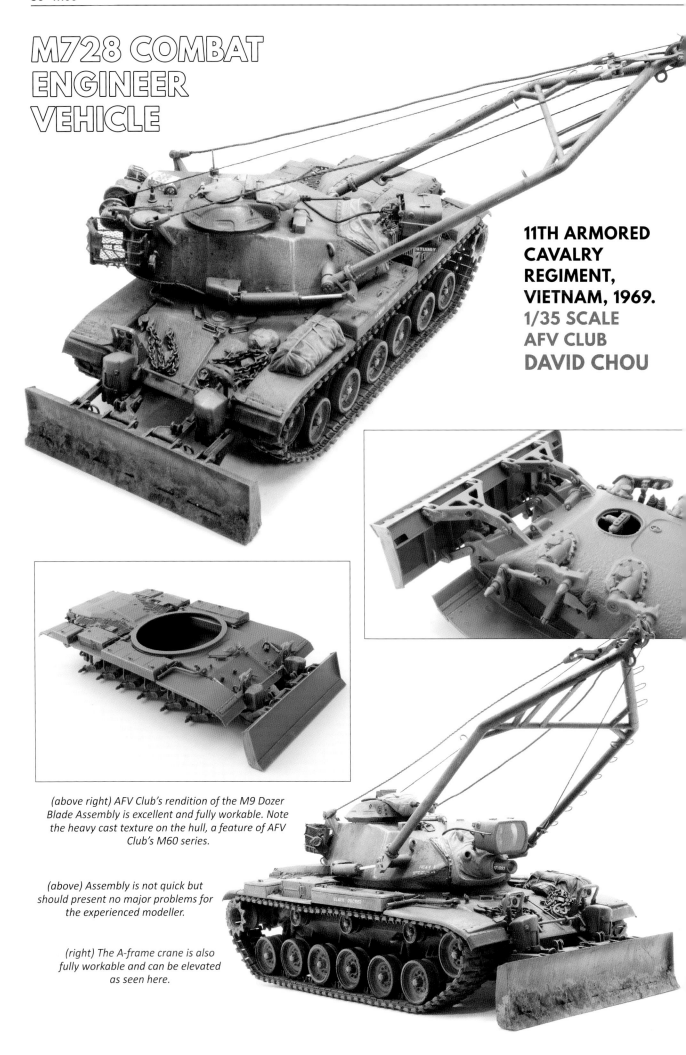

11TH ARMORED CAVALRY REGIMENT, VIETNAM, 1969.
1/35 SCALE
AFV CLUB
DAVID CHOU

(above right) AFV Club's rendition of the M9 Dozer Blade Assembly is excellent and fully workable. Note the heavy cast texture on the hull, a feature of AFV Club's M60 series.

(above) Assembly is not quick but should present no major problems for the experienced modeller.

(right) The A-frame crane is also fully workable and can be elevated as seen here.

MODELLING PRODUCTS

As the iconic American tank of the Cold War, the M60 has been a hugely popular subject among modellers and kit manufacturers alike, with a range of models covering almost all the major variants in a variety of scales. The aim of this section is to survey the available kits and accessories and provide some helpful advice from my own experience and by synthesising the comments and experience of others to modellers who wish to tackle their own M60 project.

1/35-SCALE KITS

The growth of plastic scale modelling as a hobby in the late sixties and early seventies coincided with the heyday of the M60 and it is no surprise that the first 'proper' scale model kit of the tank, released in 1970, was by the Japanese giant Tamiya. 'U.S. Army M60A1 Medium Tank' (ref. 35028) was initially in their 1/35-scale motorised series and was also boxed the following year as a static display model. Its heritage as a motorised model resulted in a hull that has been described as resembling a piece of Swiss Cheese, which numerous holes for the various gears and levers, but, overall, it is reasonable representation of the tank. The biggest problem is the suspension, which doesn't really match the complex nature of the real thing, especially the shock absorbers around the front idler wheel. The hull rear is lacking in detail, missing, for example, the curved mud guards which curve down between the rear fenders and the drive sprocket housing. Equally, the fender braces are moulded solid when they should have several circular holes, an obvious error that requires some careful replacement with photoetched replacements. Across the model, while the dimensions are reasonably sound, the detail is rather soft, and the kit is now looking like something tooled more than fifty years ago. Tamiya's M60A1 formed the basis for a M60A2 (ref. 35128), released four years later; an M60A3 (ref. 351400), which could also be built as an M60A1 RISE Passive, in 1988; and a USMC M60A1 with Reactive Armor (ref. 35157),

(above) Tamiya 35157
(below) Italeri 6582

released in the wake of the Gulf War. These latter kits introduced some new parts, and the ERA tiles on the Gulf War M60A1 are very good, but all share the same shortcomings and omissions present in the original 1970 release. Nevertheless, they are still an affordable and accessible way to begin modelling the M60 series.

Academy's M60 series are basically licensed copies of the Tamiya M60. The first in the series to be released were the M60A3 (ref. TA060) and the 'USMC M60A1 with Passive Armor' (ref. TA999) in the early 1990s, both essentially reboxes of the Tamiya kits. In 1994 Academy released an IDF M60A1 Blazer kit both with (ref. 1367) and without (ref. 1367) a KMT-4 Mine Roller, and four years later an M60A1 with M9 Dozer (ref. 1390). In 2013 they released a very nice IDF Magach 6B Gal Batash (ref. 13281) version of the M60. It was not until 2015, however, that they released a newly tooled turret for the M60A2 (ref. 13296), combining a new M60A2 turret with 152mm Shillelagh launcher, with the older Tamiya-based hull. This is a good kit, a big improvement on the older Tamiya M60A2, although it does not compare to the AFV Club version and requires some aftermarket intervention by the serious modeller.

In 1990 the Italian company ESCI/ERTL released both an 'M60A1 Patton' (ref. 5039) and an 'M60A3 TTS Improved MBT' (ref. 5040). This tooling was a definite improvement on the Tamiya/Academy kit but was not without its issues. The suspension is much better and more accurate than the Tamiya/Academy kit – albeit far from perfect – but the link-and-length tracks don't fit well and are plagued by ejector pin marks. The fender supports are separate and moulded with the correct holes, albeit somewhat overscale, while there is a nice cast texture on the upper moulding. On the downside, the driver's hatch is moulded shut. The turret is also better detailed than its Tamiya/Academy counterpart, although there is some filler needed around the main upper/lower hull and the mantlet guard is also tricky to fit without resort to filler. The turret bustle stowage bin is also an improvement over Tamiya/Academy but more of a challenge to assemble. The ESCI/ERTL kit has been reboxed periodically by Italeri and Revell over the years, the last time with Italeri's rebox of the M60A3 (ref. 6582) in 2020. In 1991 ESCI/ERTL also released an Israeli M60A1 Blazer (ref. 5042), which was subsequently reboxed by Italeri (ref. 6391).

In 2015 Dragon Models Limited released the first of several M60 kits. Unfortunately, their M60A2 'Starship' MBT (ref. 3562) was a bit of a shocker. It's fair to say that Dragon dropped the ball with their M60 series as the kits were a mishmash of newly tooled parts and sprues shared, quite incorrectly, with their very good M48 series. There are several details missing on the turret, such as the canvas mantlet cover, but more importantly, the hull

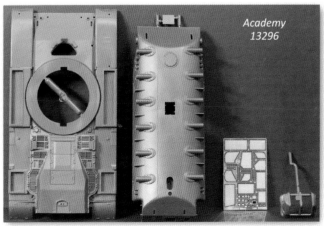

Academy 13296

(above) Dragon 3553

(above) Dragon 3591

and suspension details are something of an amalgam of features from the M48 and M60. The hull itself is several millimetres too short and too narrow, while the roadwheels are incorrectly spaced and the rear hull doors incorrect for the M60A2. The same shortcuts are evident in their M60 Patton (ref. 3553), the only available plastic kit of the 'Slick Sixty', released the following year. Several errors, such as the incorrectly spaced return rollers and inaccurate idler wheel mounts are carried over from the M60A2, but the most glaring hull problems were remedied. One of the most obvious issues with the 'Slick Sixty' kit is the main gun assembly: the 105mm gun barrel is too thin, while the characteristic mantlet cover is simply an M48 one and thus oversized. The M19 commander's cupola is also very poor, while the driver's hatch does slide as the M60's did and the AN/VSS-1 searchlight is undersized. After a couple of IDF versions with and without dozer blades (refs. 3581/3582), in 2019 Dragon released an M60 AVLB (ref. 3591), the only kit available of this vehicle in plastic or resin.

In the same year that Dragon released their M60A2, Taiwanese manufacturer AFV Club hit the market with the first of their own series of M60 kits. AFV Club's 'M60A1 Patton' (ref. AF35060) set a new standard, finally bringing modellers a 21st-century-standard M60 kit. The kit is superb: accurate and capturing a variety of details that allows the modeller to recreate a range of different M60A1 versions. The only downside to the kit is its complexity: it has over 550 olive-green plastic parts, photoetched brass, steel springs, and clear parts. The single-piece vinyl tracks are an excellent representation of the real thing. These kits are a major investment in time and will require some careful attention and are probably not for the novice builder. My only slight complaint is that the cast text on the turret is a little over done. AFV Club followed this up the next year with an early M60A2 (ref. AF35238) and M60A3/TTS (ref. AF35249), and in 2018 with a late M60A2 (ref. AF35230). In 2019 AFV Club released a superbly detailed model of the M728 Combat Engineer Vehicle (AF35254). AFV Club have also released two version of the Israeli

(above) AFV Club AF35060
(below) AFV Club AF35254

(above) AFV Club AF35238
(below) Takom 2142

The author's build of Takom's M60A3 with M9 Dozer (ref. 2137).

Magach 6B (refs. AF35309 and AF35S92). AFV Club's kit probably represent the most accurate and detailed 1/35-scale M60s on the market, but their complexity will be a challenge for some modellers.

In 2018 Chinese company Takom released a 'M60A1 w/Explosive Reactive Armor' (ref. 2113). Takom are a relatively recent name in the hobby but have quickly established a reputation for accurate and superbly moulded kits that are relatively straightforward to build. Their M60 series is no exception. The kits feature crisply moulded grey plastic, photoetch, clear parts and one-piece vinyl tracks. The kits are much easier to put together than their AFV Club counterparts and any compromise on detail is not obvious. The USMC M60A1

(RISE Passive) is particularly impressive as the ERA blocks are separate, as are their mounting brackets. Another useful inclusion is that of a jig to properly shape the photoetched mesh provided for the turret bustle stowage bin. In 2020 Takom followed this kit up with an early M60A1 (ref. 2132) and, in the following year, an M60A3 with M9 Bulldozer (ref. 2137). The latter can, of course, be built without the M9 dozer blade. The most recent release is a USMC Desert Storm 'M60A1 w/ ERA & M9 Bulldozer' (ref. 2142). Personally, I prefer the Takom M60s over the AFV Club ones, simply because of the relative ease of their assembly. Modellers can now build accurate replicas of the entire M60 series, with the notable exception of the 'Slick Sixty', through the superb AFV Club and Takom kits.

SMALLER SCALE KITS

Compared to those who work predominantly in 1/35 scale, modellers who prefer smaller scales are poorly served when it comes to the M60. In 1987 ESCI/ERTL released their 1/72-scale M60A1 (ref. 8315). This was

shortly followed by an M60A2 'Starship (ref. 8316), M60A3 (ref. 8317) and Israeli 'M60 Blazer' (ref. 8318). These kits have been variously re-issued over the years

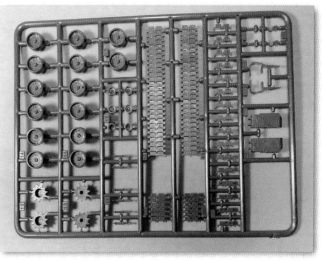

(above) ESCI/ERTL 8315
(right) Running gear sprue from ESCI/ERTL kits

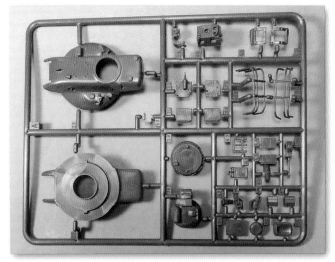

(above) Turret sprue from ESCI/ERTL 8316

(below) Revell 03140

(above) Italeri 7075

(below) Revell 03168

by AMT/ERTL in the United States, Gunze Sangyo in Japan, and most recently by Italeri. The ESCI/ERTL kits were impressive and very welcome when they were first released, but they are now beginning to show their age against the latest generation of small-scale releases. Each kit contains three olive green plastic sprues and a separate lower hull. They come with link-and-length tracks. Much of the detail is moulded on and is quite rough by today's standards. The tracks, which are the later T97 type, have some nasty sink marks. The suspension too is noticeably simplified, while the hatches are moulded shut. The turret and hull also lack the rough, cast texture, although this is easy to overdo in this scale. The ESCI/ERTL running gear is also quite basic: the drive sprockets lack the lightening holes, while the ribs on the aluminium roadwheels are indistinct. The rear stowage basket is rather poor and details like the smoke grenade launchers look poor by today's standards. The original kits are not really worth bothering with today, even if you can find them, but Italeri's 2017 re-release of the M60A1 (ref. 7075) has some renovated moulds and the detail is noticeably sharper than on the older ESCI/ERTL kits.

In 2004 Revell released a newly tooled M60A3 (ref. 03140). This kit is a marked improvement on the ESCI/ERTL effort, with sharper detail and fewer nasty injection pin marks. The hull and turret are also noticeably smaller than the ESCI/ERTL kits but scale out better when compared to drawings. Revell followed the M60A3 up three years later with an 'M60A1 with ERA' (ref. 03168) and in 2009 with an M60A3 with M9 Dozer Blade (ref. 03175). The M60A3 was reboxed with different decals in 2015. The Revell kit also includes link-and-length tracks and the later steel roadwheels. The ERA blocks on the

M60A1 are well done and the M9 Dozer is excellent for this scale. These kits are currently out of production and increasingly difficult to find but are the first choice for the small-scale modeller wishing to build a plastic M60.

There are a handful of small-scale resin kits available of the M60. Cromwell Models offered 1/72-scale resin kits of the Turkish M60T Sabra (ref. 72215), and the Israeli Magach 7C (ref. 72077) and Magach 6 Batash (ref. 72002), but none of the 'standard' M60 variants. Similarly, Modell Trans Modelbau have a Magach 6 Early (M60 Blazer) (ref. 72229) in their catalogue but no American tanks. We can only hope that companies like Takom or Border Model can be tempted to include a newly tooled M60 in their future catalogues.

(below) Revell 03175

CONVERSIONS, DETAILS SETS AND ACCESSORIES

CONVERSION SETS

Given that the ESCI/ERTL and Tamiya/Academy kits were the only 1/35-scale kits of the M60 on the market for many years, there are surprisingly few conversions and update sets available. The notable gap in the 1/35-scale kit catalogue, as already noted, is the 'Slick Sixty' and a couple of companies offer resin conversions to convert the existing plastic kits to the earlier variant. Korean firm DEF Model produce an 'M60 Patton Conversion Set' (ref. DM35025) designed for the Tamiya/Academy kit and which includes a new resin turret, gun mantlet and searchlight, as well as a set of AFV Club T97E2 tracks and a turned metal barrel. This is an excellent set and can result in superb model, as Uwe Kern shows in the gallery section. Legend Productions also produced an M60 conversion kit with new resin turret, mantlet, searchlight and gun barrel (ref. LF1130). Legend Productions also produce several resin kits to convert the standard American gun tanks into later versions of the Israeli Magach 6 and 7 tanks. Similar conversions are also offered by the German maker, MR Models, who also do a conversion of the Italeri M60A3 to a Turkish Sabra M60A3 (ref. 35059).

Another Korean company, Adler, released a range of high-quality conversion sets designed to improve the existing plastic kits in the early 2010s. These were a new M60A1/A3 hull (ref. 35080), a detailed M60A1/A3 turret conversion (ref. 35079), and a new turret and rear panel to produce an M60A2 (ref. 35076). These were very good but are not out of production and virtually impossible to find. The same is true of the range of conversions offered by US-based manufacturer AEF Designs. This included several sets designed to convert the Tamiya/Academy kit to several Israeli tanks, an M60A2 and an M60A1 with reactive armour. Another US company, also long gone, was Chesapeake Designs who did a very nice M60 resin turret conversion (ref. CMD-15). Before the advent of AFV Club's M728 AEV several companies offered resin conversions. These included Adler (ref. 35072), A.E.F. Deigns (ref. RA-602), R&J Products (ref. HK-35.1701) and Perfect Scale Modellbau (refs. 35052 and 35099

with dozer blade).

For modellers who prefer working in smaller scales Black Dog offer a 1/72 resin Magach 6B conversion for the Revell kit (ref. T72066). MR Models also do a M60 conversion for the Revell kit including turret, M19 commander's cupola and stowed rear turret bustle rack (ref. MR-72104), while Modell Trans Modellbau produce resin conversions for the M60A2 (ref. MT72122), Marksman AA Turret (MT72508), Taiwanese CM-11 'Brave Tiger' (ref. MT72185), Magach 6 (MT72211) and M728 (ref. MT72180).

INDIVIDUAL TRACK LINKS

The vinyl tracks included in the original Tamiya/Academy kits and the ESCI/ERTL link-and-length tracks were quite poor and it is no surprise that a range of manufacturers offer replacement tracks for the available 1/35-scale M60 kits. For those modellers who prefer metal individual links Friulmodel do a set of T-142 tracks (ref. ATL-143) and T97E2 links (ATL-142), while Spade Ace Models offer both T97 (ref. SAT-35139) and T142 (ref. SAT-35138) tracks. Both consist of single links comprising track pads and end connectors, but for those modellers wanting extra detail they also produce a set with separate track pads, end connectors and guide horns (ref. SAT-35183S). R Model also produce a T142 set (ref. 35138) which is, essentially, a copy of the Friul set. For those who prefer plastic, multi-part tracks, AFV Club produce both T142 (ref. AF3510) and T97 (ref. AF3505) tracks. These consist of individual links that click together and are held in place by the end connectors which simply push over the track pins moulded into each link. No glue is required, and they remain completely workable after assembly. The AFV Club T142 tracks were also boxed by DEF Model (ref. DA35002). In terms of resin tracks, Slingshotmodels, a small Greek manufacturer, produced an interesting set of Turkish T517 tracks for the Sabra (ref. SSM35006). In small scale, OKB Grigorov produce a set of resin T97E2 tracks (ref. P72002) designed to fit their replacement wheels for the ESCI and Revell kits (ref. S72421 Late and S72209 Early), while MR Models have in their catalogue

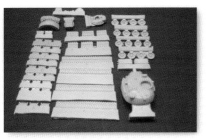

(above) DEF Model DM35025
(below) MR Models MR72014

(above) Adler 35076
(above right) Black Dog T72066
(below right) Friulmodel ATL-142
(below) Modell Trans Modellbau MT72180

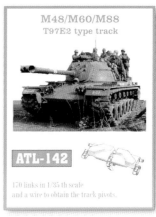

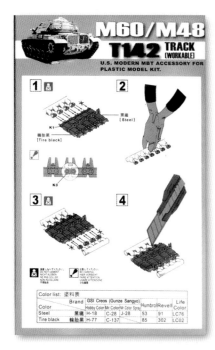

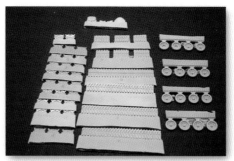

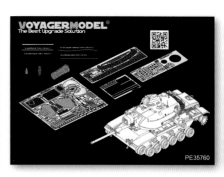

(above) MR Models MR-72109
(above right) Voyager Model PE35760
(right) DEF Model DM35001

(above) AFV Club AF3510
(right) Voyager Model PE351028

a complete set of replacement resin roadwheels and T97 link-and-length tracks for the Revell kit (ref. MR-72109).

DETAIL SETS

Again, given their age it is no surprise that a variety of aftermarket manufacturers have come up with a range of replacement parts, in both resin and photoetch, to improve and detail the Tamiya/Academy and ESCI/ERTL M60 kits. There is a good range of photoetched detail sets for the older kits and models of this vintage lend themselves to the type of improvements a photoetched brass set can include. A case in point is the moulded in solid fender supports of the older Tamiya/Academy kits. This area of the kit can be improved by carefully removing the moulded-on detail and replacing it with correctly scaled and detailed photoetched brass. That said, photoetch has its limitations: it involves basically bending two-dimensional sheet of brass into three-dimensional shapes and the material can be difficult to work with if you don't have access to proper bending tools.

Czech company Eduard were one of the first to popularise the use of photoetched details sets among armour modellers and their releases of the early 2000s contained several sets for the Academy, Italeri and Tamiya M60s. These included for sets for the Tamiya M60A1 (ref. 35431), Academy M60A1 (ref. 35448), Italeri M60 Blazer (ref. 35467) and Italeri M60A1 (ref. 35725). These were all similar in design, including stowage basket mesh, rear mud deflectors, fender supports and a host of other details. Eduard's armour releases have slowed of late but in 2020 they released a sheet for the Takom M60A1 (ref. 36453), although any improvements over the kit parts would be marginal for all but the most diehard exponent of photoetched brass.

Chinese company Voyager have taken a more involved approach to providing photoetched details sets for armour modellers. Their sets often include several sheets of photoetch of different thicknesses, as well as resin, brass, and other metal components. They have released extensive set for the AFV Club (ref. PE35760) and Takom (ref. PE351160) M60A1s, as well as for the AFV Club M728 (ref. PE351028). However, the relative

lack of photoetched detail sets for the latest generation of plastic kits shows just how good these recent releases are.

Other companies have taken a different approach to improving the older M60 kits, offering resin replacements for many of the poorly detailed kit parts. DEF Model lead the way in this with a generic resin update set for Tamiya/Academy which includes new front mudguards, fender supports and a new rear plate (ref. DM35002). They also produce a resin, photoetched and brass rod set to update the turret of any of the older 1/35-scale plastic kits (ref. DM35001). Perhaps best of all from DEF Model is a very nice multi-media set to update the Academy M60A2 (ref. DM35056). These sets are complemented by a selection of turned metal and resin barrels: early (ref. DM35063) and late (ref. DM35061) barrels for the M60A2; early (ref. DM35106) and late (ref. DM35105) barrels and wind sensors for the M60A3; a replacement for the inaccurate barrel in the Dragon M60 kit (ref. DM35082); and a metal barrel for the AFV Club M60A1 (ref. DM35073). The M60A3 barrel sets have been re-released and updated with some additional parts recently (refs. DM35016A and 15A).

Legend Productions are another company with a wide range of resin-based updates sets for the M60 family in their category. Many of these relate to Israeli versions of the tank, but modellers whose interest is in American and European vehicles will want to consider the M60 Tank Cupola (ref. LF1249). This is a superb resin kit of the M19 commander's cupola and includes a full interior. Legend also offers a nicely detailed AVDS-1790 Engine and Compartment Set (ref. LF1344) and an engine and sling set (LF1343), perfect for a maintenance vignette or diorama. There is also a separate and specific engine set for the AFV Club kit (ref. LF1341), as well as an older M60A3 engine (ref. LF1030). There is also a generic detailing set for the Tamiya M60A1/A3 (ref. LF1248), which contains the cupola set, new mantlet and main gun, front mudguards, and other details. To give your M60A1 or A3 a suitably lived-in look, Legend also has 'M60A1 Sandbag Armor/MRE Box Set' (ref. LF1181) and 'M60A1 Stowage Set' (ref. LF1169). The former is perfect for modelling a USMC Gulf War tank, while the latter

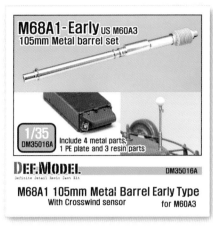

(above) DEF Model DM35001

(below) Legend Productions LF1344

(above) DEF Model DM35056

(above) Legend Productions LF1249

(left) SOL MM309

includes a selection of various ALICE packs, jerry cans and other stowage items. The resin is superbly cast, but as with all similar sets, will need some basic modelling skills to fit convincingly onto the tank.

Various other companies have offered M60 family accessories and updates over the past two decades or so and many are now out of production. It is still possible to obtain the various resin accessories and detail sets offered by SOL. These include stowage sets for the M60A2 (ref. MM309) and M60A1/A3 (ref. MM207), as well as the excellent M60A1/A3 turret previously released under the Adler label (ref. MM209). Elefant Corporation is a relatively new manufacturer of resin accessories based in the UK. In their catalogue they offer replacement aluminium (ref. 35133) and steel (ref. 35129) roadwheels. These are multi-part efforts with separate hubs, but the detail is second-to-none. They also offer a set of replacement and finely detailed fuel caps for the M60 family (ref. 35045). Also worth mentioning are the 3D-printed accessories by Spanish company FC Modeltrend. These include a superb but very delicate rear basket for the M60A1/A3 (ref. 35788), a set of replacement shackles and handles (ref. 35762) and M60 tow cables (ref. 35862). The latter simply

needed gently heating in hot water or with a hair dryer and then moulding to shape on the model. Finally, there is a set of Spanish smoke grenade launchers as fitted to their M60A3s (ref. 35442). Panzer Art also produced a set of nicely cast resin aluminium roadwheels for the M60 (ref. RE35-129).

In the smaller scales there are a few detail sets available. Both OKB Grigorov (ref. P72003) and Hauler (ref. HLH72046) produce photoetched detail sets for the Revell M60 series. Black Dog do a very nice set of resin stowage and sandbag armour (ref. T72017) designed for the Revell M60A1 but which, as you can see in the gallery, can be employed on any small-scale M60 model.

DECALS

Given the long and varied service of the M60, there are relatively few decal sets available to replace those supplied in the various plastic kits. Echelon Fine Details produce three sets of decals for the M60A3 which include a nice range of US Army, OPFOR and European marking options (refs. D3562541, D356240, D356238). FC Modeltrend produce a comprehensive sheet for Spanish Army and Marines M60A3 (ref. 35217). Finally, LM Decals produced a sheet for the M60A1 and A3 in Hellenic service (ref. LM35013).

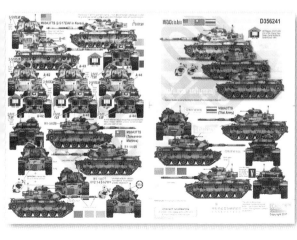

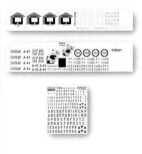

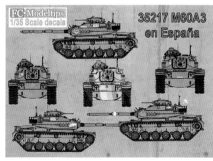

(left, above)
Echelon Fine Details
D3562541

(above) FC Modeltrend 35217

Continued from page 15...

1964 four prototype turrets were proposed for testing: two were of a revolutionary low-silhouette design with a 20mm coaxial cannon (dubbed Types A and B), while two were based on the M60A1E1 (Types C and D), the first of these also featuring a 20mm cannon housed in the commander's cupola. The Type B turret was selected for further development and designated the M60A1E1. Two prototypes were built between October 1965 and February the following year and subjected to a host of engineering and development tests, including firing 23 Shillelagh missiles from the gun-launcher. All but three launches were successful, confirming the suitability of the new turret for the proposed sea change in US armour development. In December 1965 Chrysler had been awarded a contract to produce turret components and in May 1966 limited production of the M60A1E1 was approved.

The project was soon in trouble, however. Although it had been given Standard A classification for the missile – standardised as the Surface Attack Guided Missile MGM-51A Shillelagh – in November 1966, the new gun-launcher was far from ready for service. Problems with the combustible-case ammunition included misfire and premature detonation, while the smouldering residue of the previous round presented a deadly danger to the crew when loading the next round. The rounds were easily damaged in transit and were adversely affected by high humidity. The crews charged with testing the new ammunition had little confidence in it. Nevertheless, in 1968 the Army, aware of the lack of firepower in armoured cavalry regiments in Vietnam, approved the 152mm gun-launcher and the M551 Sheridan for service.

(above) Preventive Maintenance Monthly introduces the M60A2 to new crewmen in April 1975 in its own inimitable style. (US Army)

Indeed, it would be November 1971 before the gun-launcher-armed M60 was standardised as the Tank, Combat, Full-Tracked: 152mm Gun Launcher M60A2. The five years between the approval of low-run production and the award to Chrysler of a contract to retrofit the new turret on M60A1 hulls witnessed extensive testing and improvements to ready the new tank for service. In October 1970 a final prototype, the M60A1E2, was built and between December that year and September 1971 some 338 test firings of the 152mm gun-launcher took place. New turrets were left waiting in the Chrysler factory in Warren, Michigan, while industrial action delayed delivery of the new tanks and it was not until February 1973 that the first M60A2 was delivered to the US Army. In all Chrysler produced a total of 526 vehicles (although US Army sources claim 540). The first 243 turrets were fitted to existing M60A1 hulls fitted with the TLAC, while the remainder were newly built tanks until production ceased in 1975. The M60A2 carried fifteen rounds of 152mm ammunition and seven of the new Shillelagh MGM-51C missiles for its XM162E1 gun-launcher in the turret, with eighteen conventional rounds and six missiles were stored in the hull. It was armed with a coaxial M73 7.62mm machine and had the M19 cupola mounting the M85 .50cal machine gun.

It took until February 1975 for the first M60A2 to arrive with the US 7th Army in Germany, equipping B Company, 1-32 Armor. In all, six armour battalions were eventually equipped with the M60A2: 5-68 Armor, 8th Infantry Division (54 M60A2); 1-32 Armor and 3-33 Armor, 3rd Armored

(above) Another spread from the same magazine discusses the issues around the Closed Breach Scavenging System. (US Army)

Division (54 M60A2 each); 1-64 Armor, 4-64 Armor (17 M60A2 each) and 2-64 Armor and 3-64 Armor, 3rd Infantry Division (37 M60A2 each); and 1-37 Armor, 1st Armored Division (54 M60A2). Additionally, two units – 1-67 Armor, 1st Cavalry Division (54 M60A2) and 2-6 Armored Cavalry, US Armor School (17 M60A2) – fielded the tank in the United States.

In service the problems of the M60A2 became apparent. The issue of the smouldering debris from the combustible-case ammunition was solved by the Closed Breach Scavenging System (CBSS). This delivered three blasts of compressed air, contained in large tanks installed in a bulge just below the louvre doors at the rear of the vehicle, to clear any dangerous residues. This proved successful and later-production M60A2 omitted the bore evacuator on the gun tube. More damning was the lack of night vision equipment and the fact that the small turret prevented the installation of a stereoscopic rangefinder. The lack of night vision necessitated the use of the xenon searchlight and a pink filter which extended the range to 1,000m. As the Shillelagh was ineffective at ranges less than 1,000m, this meant that the tank's primary armament was virtually useless at night (although it could fire conventional ammunition).

The M60A2 was neither popular among its crews nor an effective weapon of war. The Shillelagh missile was prone to malfunctions and rarely fired. The Army's Preventive Maintenance Monthly of April 1975 introduced the latest weapons in its arsenal to the new crewmen. It heralded the M60A2 as major improvement over the M60A1: 'my design keeps me low in the saddle and my hardware is red hot and rarin' to go. With all the improvements in tank turret design, I can out-shoot and out-fight any hombre on the range.' It did warn prospective crewmen, however, to read their manuals carefully lest they 'foul up' the parts that made the M60A2 a 'super tank'. The small turret, the periodical warned, meant 'space is limited.' Crew members with big feet needed to be careful lest they 'kick the gunner's panel – it really smarts and knocks my firing and alinement mechanisms outta whack.' Indeed, climbing in and out of the tank required acts of contortion to prevent damaging the fragile new equipment. The CBSS needed regular maintenance and application of the correct oil to work properly, while the airlines contained 3,000psi of compressed air that remained in the system when it was shut down, providing a nasty 'surprise for the unwary.' The combustible-case ammunition also required special care, while the Fire Control System was difficult to use and the cable for the infrared beam used to direct the Shillelagh missile to its target easily damaged.

By the late 1970s tank technology had moved on again and the missile firing M60A2 was obsolete. The Shillelagh missile was inadequate against the latest generation of the Soviet tanks, the T-64 and T-72, and was eventually replaced with the BGM-71 TOW, first introduced in 1971. By 1979 the number of armor battalions equipped with the tank in Germany had been reduced to three. By 1982 it had been withdrawn from service and the turrets scrapped. Some M60A2 hulls were converted to M60 Armored Vehicle Launched Bridge (AVLB), while others became M60A3 gun tanks.

M60A3

As we have seen, during 1972 and 1973 twelve M60A1E3 prototypes were built which featured all the improvements of the M60A1 programme (AOS, RISE and Passive), as well as a laser range finder. During the next five years the changes incorporated into production M60A1s were also included in the prototypes and in May 1979 this version was standardised as the Tank, Combat, Full Tracked: 105mm Gun, M60A3. The new tank had been in production before standardisation and the first vehicles entered service with 1-32 Armor in Germany in the same month. There were three main changes that differentiated the M60A3 from the late-production M60A1 (RISE Passive). These were the thermal shroud fitted to the 105mm gun (which received the new designation M68A1), the armoured top-loading air cleaners, and most significantly the Laser Tank Fire Control System (LT-FTS). This latter system consisted of two main components: the AN/VVG-2 fire control laser rangefinder and the solid-state M21 ballistic computer. The AN/VVG-2 replaced the M17C rangefinder and had an operational range of up to 4,700m. The M21 was a major step forward and increased the tank's lethality considerably. The computer corrected for crosswind (measured by a prominent sensor at the rear of the turret roof), ammunition characteristics, target speed, altitude, air temperature, the condition and age of the M68A1 gun, gun sight parallax and trunnion cant. The AN/VVG-2 had a characteristic bulge on the right-side of the turret for the viewfinder, another useful feature in identifying the M60A3 TTS. Other improvements, also found on late-production M60A1 (RISE Passive) included the M240 coaxial machine, M239 grenade launchers, and the VEESS.

Much of the effort spent during the late 'seventies with the M60A1E3 prototypes and on the M60 improvement programme generally was in developing a new system of suspension. Both the Tube over Bar suspension and new aluminium torsion bars were trialled but found to offer minimal advantages over the existing suspension. Changes were introduced, however, into the tank's running gear with the M60A3. In 1980 the ribbed aluminium roadwheels and return rollers were replaced with steel ones, which were also retrofitted to many M60A1s. Other production improvements included, from 1984, a new Vehicle Exhaust Dust Ejector System that replaced the previous air cleaner centrifugal fans.

More significantly, 1980 also saw the introduction of the AN/VSG-2 Tank Thermal Sight (TTS) which replaced the gunner's M35E1 periscope daylight/passive sight. The TTS enabled the M60A3 to operate effectively in all conditions and see through fog, smoke and exhaust fumes. This placed the M60A3 TTS, as tanks so equipped were designated, on a par with third generation MBTs, such as the M1 Abrams, West German Leopard 2 and Soviet T-80, at least in terms of lethality.

In 1980 the M1 Abrams entered service and the M60 began to be phased out of service with the frontline units of the US Army. US armour doctrine was changing too and with the introduction of the Bradley Fighting Vehicle the following year, the evolution of the concept of the AirLand Battle, and a new structure for the US Army's armoured divisions, the M60's days were numbered. It was not, however, until 1987

An M60A3 TTS of 3-32 Armor, 3rd (US) Armored Division during Exercise Central Guardian 85. In this exercise M60A3 TTS still equipped most of the US Army's armour battalions. (US Army photo by SSgt. Fernando Serna)

that production of the M60A3 TTS ceased at the Detroit Arsenal Tank Plant. By then 1,868 new M60A3s had been produced, while some 3,700 M60A1 tanks had been upgraded to M60A3 standard.

The withdrawal of the M60A3 from service with the US Army was a slow process. The final M60s were retired from the USAEUR in 1989/90, where they still served in the divisional reconnaissance battalions, while the last regular unit based in the US – 2-7 Cavalry, the divisional reconnaissance battalion of 4th Infantry Division (Mechanized) – swapped its M60A3 TTS for Bradley Fighting Vehicles in 1992. The Army National Guard continued to operate the M60A3 TTS until 1998. Even this was not the end of the M60A3 TTS, however. It continued to be operated by the Armor

(above) Another M60A3 TTS of 4-69 Armor, 8th (US) Infantry Division (Mechanized) during Exercise Central Guardian. During this exercise, held in January 1985, 8th Infantry Division played the role of Blue Forces. The white '76' on a blue background is the Blue Force unit identifier. (US Army photo by SSgt. David Nolan)

Company of 1-4 Infantry, the OPFOR unit at the Combat Maneuver Training Center at Hohenfels in Bavaria. The three tank platoons, each with ten M60A3 TTS, along with three in the battalion HQ, represented T-80s of '4th Guards Motorized Rifle Regiment', while modified M113A2 represented BMP-2s. The M60A3 TTS remained in service in this role until 2005 when Combat Maneuver Training Center was redesignated the Joint Multinational Readiness Center.

An M60A3 TTS of 1-108 Armor, a unit of the Georgia Army National Guard, during Exercise Team Defense '83 held at Fort Stewart, GA. (US Army photo by SSgt. Long)

M60 VARIANTS: M60 AVLB AND M728

There were two main variants of the M60: the M728 Combat Engineer Vehicle (CEV) and the Armored Vehicle Launched Bridge (AVLB). The development of a new CEV began in the late 'fifties. In 1962 it was decided to fit the hydraulic crane system and the 165mm XM135 cannon, based on the British L9A1 gun, to the hull and turret of the M60A1. The four-man crew was situated as they were in the gun tank and the CEV was equipped with the M19 cupola and its .50 calibre machine gun. The CEV was also equipped with an 'A' frame boom with a lifting capacity of 17,500lbs, a 25,000lbs capacity winch, the M9 dozer blade and a 2.2kw xenon searchlight. The three prototypes were standardised as the Full Tracked, Combat Engineer Vehicle M278 in November 1965. A total of 243 CEVs were produced in Detroit between 1966 and 1972 and it saw action in the Vietnam War and the Gulf War, as well as serving in the peace-keeping missions in the Balkans in the 1990s.

The idea of bridge-laying tanks had been explored by the US Army in the years immediately after the end of World War II and in the late 'fifties several M48A2C tanks were fitted with scissor bridges designed to span gaps of forty and sixty feet. The M60 was adapted to this use from 1964 with Chrysler producing 393 AVLBs on the M60A1 chassis between 1964 and 1981. The M60 AVLB also saw action in the Vietnam and Gulf wars and is the only vehicle based on the M60 chassis that is still in service with the US Army today.

An M278 uses its M9 bulldozer to good effect. Note the large A-frame boom and the prominent AN/VSS-1 searchlight. (US Army photo by Don Teft)

The 2nd Armored Brigade Combat Team, 1st Infantry Division train with the M60 AVLB in Korea in February 2020. (US Army photo by SSgt. Simon McTizic)

M60 IN FOREIGN SERVICE

The M60 has seen extensive service in the armed forces of over 25 nations beside those of the United States. The users can broadly be divided into two categories: those countries that received M60s in the 1960s and 70s, while the tank was still a state-of-the-art MBT, and those that received them in the 80s and 90s, as the US phased out the M60 in favour of the M1 Abrams.

The most important foreign user of the M60 was, of course, Israel. The Israel Defense Forces (IDF) first purchased M60A1 tanks from the US in the wake of the Six-Day War in 1967. These were modified for Israeli use with the locally produced Urdan low-profile commander's cupola and Blazer ERA, and designated Magach 6 in Israeli service. On the eve of the Yom Kippur War in 1973, the IDF had some 540 Magach 3 (based on the M48A3) and Magach 6 in its inventory but suffered over 300 losses during the conflict. This stock was supplemented after the war by further imports of M60A1 and older M60s. The latter received the AVCR-1790-5A engine, armour and fire control upgrades, and eventually the tracks from the Israeli Merkava MBT. They were known as Magach 7. The Magach 6 and 7 went through a series of upgrades until they were finally withdrawn from active service in 2014.

Another important early user of the M60 was Iran. Iran signed a deal for M60s as early as 1969 and in total 460 M60A1s were transferred before the Islamic Revolution and the overthrow of the Shah in 1979. The tanks were fully assembled and modified at the Masjed received a coaxial .50cal machine gun, as well as other small modifications. The M60A1 fought with distinction in the Iran-Iraq War and over a hundred were destroyed in action. After the war ended in 1988, the remaining Iranian M60A1s were upgraded. The 'Samsam' (Sword) was fitted Soviet-style ERA, a new fire control and early warning anti-ATGM system, as well as IR jammers. Others were cannibalised for parts for the prototype 'Zulfiqar' tank. In 2010 an estimated 150 M60A1s were still in service with the Iranian armed forces.

Between 1974 and 1977 160 M60A1 were sold to Ethiopia, where they served until being replaced with East German T-72s at the end of the decade when their longstanding cooperation with the United States ended, while Sudan purchased twenty M60A1 in 1979. Italy produced 200 M60A1 under licence and received a further 100 from surplus US stocks in Europe during the late 1970s. In the 1980s the number of countries using the M60 grew. Morocco first purchased the M60A1 in 1981, receiving 108 tanks. It then purchased 300 ex-USMC M60A1 between 1991 and 1994 and a further 120 M60A1 and M60A3 TTS between 1994 and 1997. Taiwan was another important user of the

(below) An Iranian M60A1 of the 92nd Armoured Division in Khuzestan Province during the early days of the Iran-Iraq War. (Vorya Heidaryan)

M60, receiving several hundred M60A3 TTS in the 1980s, converting some 400 to the CM-11 Brave Tiger, which uses the M48A3 turret with the M60A3 hull and M1 Abrams fire control system. Other countries, such as Greece, Spain and Portugal, received surplus US stock from 1991 under the Conventional Forces in Europe Treaty. They remained in service until replaced by the Leopard 2 in the 2010s.

The most important users of the M60 today are Egypt, Turkey and Saudi Arabia. As of 2019, Egypt had 1,150, Turkey some 916 and Saudi Arabia 390 M60s of various designations. Egypt purchased 1,600 M60A3 TTS and 700 M60A1 RISE tanks form the US between 1986 and 2002. Attempts to upgrade the fleet by mating a T-55 turret to the M60A1 RISE hull proved unsuccessful. Turkey acquired large number of M60s in the early 1990s. In the late 1990s Turkey sought to modernise its M60 fleet and in 2002 a contract was signed with the Israel Military Industries to modernise 170 M60A3 as the Sabra Mk. 2. The Sabra is basically an upgraded version of the Magach 7 with new engine, ERA and conventional armour packages, and Merkava tracks. It is known as the M60T in Turkish service and first saw action against Kurdish militants in northern Syria in 2016. The Turkish Army is currently developing its own Sabra Mk. 3 upgrade

(below) An M60A3 TTS of the Spanish Infanteria de Marina during Exercise Bright Star held in Egypt in October 2001. (US Air Force photo by SRA. D Myles Curran)

which will feature the Commander's Remote Operated Weapons System (CROWS) and locally developed fire control system and commander's independent thermal viewer. Interestingly, and controversially, in April 2021 Turkey also appears to have delivered some of its old stock of M60A1 to the Government of National Accord in Libya in contravention of the United Nations arms embargo on the North African state. Saudi Arabia acquired 910 M60A1 RISE from the late 1970s, subsequently upgrading many of them to M60A3 TTS standard. In 1990 the Kingdom purchased a further 390 M60A3 TTS. The Saudi M60s saw action in the 1991 Gulf War and during the war in Yemen and some 200 M60A1 were transferred to the government of North Yemen. It is estimated that around fifty Saudi M60s have been lost in action, mainly to ATGMs, in Yemen.

There have also been several, largely unsuccessful, attempts to develop modernisation packages for the large numbers of M60s still in the inventories of armies around the world. Israeli firms Raytheon and Elbit Systems have offered such upgrades, as has the Italian firm Leonardo DRS. Other attempts to breathe life into the venerable M60, such as General Dynamics Land Division's M60-2000 hybrid using parts from the M1 Abrams, have not gone into production. Nevertheless, as of 2019 over 3,600 M60A1 and M60A3 remained in service with the armed forces of seventeen nations from Bahrain and Bosnia-Herzegovina to Thailand and Tunisia, testimony to one of the most successful tank design programmes of the twentieth century.

M60 CAMOUFLAGE AND MARKINGS

Throughout World War II until the mid 1970s, US Army tanks, indeed all military vehicles, were painted Olive Drab. The M60 was no exception. This simple statement obscures the rather complex history of Olive Drab and the camouflage and markings applied to the M60 tank throughout its long service history. The Lustreless Olive Drab applied to US vehicles during the war (A/N 319 or US Army Ground Forces (AGF) QM Color 22) was standardised in March 1956 as Federal Standard (FS) 34087 (or FS24807 in semi-gloss and FS14807 in gloss). In 1960 a new shade of FS34087 was introduced which was lighter and more yellow than the previous one. In 1968 Olive Drab was revisited again and the new shade of FS34087 did not match its predecessors, being both lighter and browner in hue than before. M60 tanks, then, appeared in at least three authorised shades of Olive Drab between 1960 and the early 1970s, with subtle variations occasioned by the differences in the paint's application, maintenance and environmental conditions.

'Camouflage', the 1968 US Field Manual on the subject stated, 'is one of the basic weapons of war. Correctly used, it can spell the difference between a successful campaign and defeat.' From the late 1960s American military planners once again turned their attention to developing a multi-colour vehicle camouflage. In 1968 a new field manual contained a card listing the latest Federal Standard colours available for vehicle camouflage, but it was not until 1972 that two US Army agencies – the Mobility Equipment Research and Development Center (MERDC) at Fort Belvoir, Virginia and the Modern Army Selected Systems Test, Evaluation and Review (MASSTER) at Fort Hood, Texas – began to officially test and evaluate new vehicle camouflage patterns. Trials took place with units of the 2nd Armored and 1st Cavalry Divisions at Fort Hood. The 1974 MERDC report noted that few soldiers had any aptitude for painting camouflage patterns, but with a little training they could competently apply relatively complex patterns with both a brush and a spray gun. The report concluded though that 'camouflage pattern painting is an effective camouflage technique which reduces visual and near infrared ground target acquisition from ground or air observations' and recommended the application of multi-colour patterned camouflage in semi-gloss enamel paint for military vehicles.

Alongside the tests on vehicle camouflage carried out in the United States, units of the US Seventh Army based in Germany also began trials. These may have predated those begun by MERDC and MASSTER, and in 1973 units of Seventh Army began to appear on exercise sporting new camouflage patterns. This pattern is commonly, although erroneously, known as the MASSTER pattern. The colours to be used were set down in USAEUR Regulation 5-525. They were Rust Brown (FS30117) and Sand (FS30372), each covering 40 per cent of the vehicle's service, and Forest Green (FS34079) and Black (FS37038) covering the remaining 20 per cent. The camouflage pattern was to be applied at unit level, using either a spray gun or a brush. All markings, both national and bumper codes, were to be applied in black. Templates were supplied, certainly for the M60A1, showing the correct pattern to be painted on vehicles and, if the later Technical Bulletin 43-0147 (issued in 1977 for the MERDC scheme) is any guide, the pattern was to be drawn onto the vehicle using chalk, each area numbered, and the pattern filled in according to the number assigned to each camouflage colour. Whatever the regulations, it is clear that there was considerable variation in the application of the MASSTER scheme across

An M60 painted in overall Olive Drab FS34087, displays an interesting set of markings, including a yellow tactical marking and the bore evacuator painted white. (Hans Stenzel via Carl Schulze)

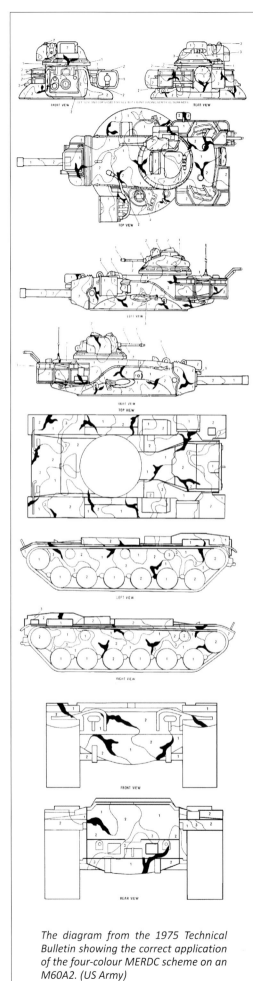

The diagram from the 1975 Technical Bulletin showing the correct application of the four-colour MERDC scheme on an M60A2. (US Army)

the units of US Seventh Army during the 1970s. There are plenty of examples of AFVs and softskins painted in a three-colour scheme using Rust Brown, Sand and Forest Green, and there are instances of bumper codes being applied in white.

The MASSTER scheme was only one of the experimental schemes employed in USAEUR during the 1970s. From 1978 vehicles of the 2nd Armored Cavalry Regiment were painted in the DUALTEX (Dual Texture Gradient Pattern) pattern, a complex grid pattern of 100mm squares of Forest Green, Sand, Field Drab and Black, reminiscent of the digital camouflage patterns of today.

The 1974 MERDC report recommended the adoption of a four-colour camouflage pattern for all military vehicles and helicopters and in December 1975 this was standardised in the Technical Bulletin 43-0147 'Color, Marking and Camouflage Patterns used on Military Equipment'. This set out both the colours to be used and the pattern of application. Seven four-colour schemes were specified each containing two major colours (covering 45 per cent of the vehicle surface each) and two minor colours (each covering five per cent). Twelve different colours were authorised for use: White (FS37875), Desert Sand (FS32079), Earth Yellow (FS30257), Earth Red (FS30117), Field Drab (FS30118), Earth Brown (FS30099), Olive Drab (FS34087), Light Green (F34151), Dark Green (FS34102), Forest Green (FS34079) and Black (FS 37038). The patterns would remain the same, but by substituting one or two colours the camouflage used could be adapted to environment and season. The schemes were as follows, with the first two colours covering 90 per cent and the two supplementary colours covering ten per cent.

Winter Verdant: Forest Green, Field Drab, Desert Sand and Black

Summer Verdant: Forest Green, Light Green, Desert Sand and Black

Tropical: Forest Green, Dark Green, Light Green and Black

Snow, Temperate Open Terrain: White, Field Drab, Sand and Black

Snow, Temperate with Trees: Forest Green, White, Sand and Black

Grey Desert: Sand, Field Drab, Earth Yellow and Black

Red Desert: Earth Red, Earth Yellow, Sand and Black

An eighth scheme for use in Arctic conditions saw the vehicles covered entirely in White.

The MERDC scheme was adopted by both the US Army and the US Army and remained current until the standard NATO three-colour scheme (Green FS34094, Brown FS30051 and Black FS37030) was adopted in 1984. There were, of course, variations to the strictly defined MERDC scheme and not all M60s were painted

A vehicle park of USMC M60A1 (RISE) in September 1981 freshly painted in the Grey Desert MERDC scheme of Sand, Field Drab, Earth Yellow and Black. (USMC photo by Sgt. M.E. Weatherington)

according to the 1975 regulations. Many of the M60s held in POMCUS (Prepositioning of Materiel Configured in Unit Sets) in Germany were painted in an overall Forest Green finish, while some USMC vehicles may have been painted in the distinctive US Marine Corps Green FS35042 when first taken into service. US Army National Guard unit M60s were also sometimes finished in a single colour during the 1980s, either Forest Green or the new NATO Green. Some M60A3 in Germany and USMC M60A1s were repainted in the new NATO scheme in 1984, but others soldiered on in their MERDC schemes until they were withdrawn from service. In 1991 the USMC M60A1s that took part in the first Gulf War were given a coat of Tan FS33446 or, possibly Sand FS33303, at the port of Al Jubayl in Saudi Arabia (where they also

had their ERA fitted).

The markings on the M60 followed the regulations for other US armoured vehicles. These consisted of principally the vehicle registration number, prefixed by 'US Army' and stencilled in Lustreless White on the fender stowage bins, and the unit identification on the front glacis and rear of the vehicle. This consisted of the unit name and an inverted equilateral triangle to denote an armoured unit, as well as the platoon and vehicle number. In the 1960s M60s were also occasionally marked with white stars, as well as tactical numbers on the turret. A whole range of other markings, such as the blue and orange unit markings used in the annual REFORGER exercises or the vehicle names applied to USMC M60A1s in the Gulf War, were applied from time to time.

An M60A1 (RISE Passive) finished in the experimental DualTex scheme sits outside Rhein-Main Airbase in September 1985. (National Archives)

M60A1 WALKAROUND

This unmodified M60A1 now stands at the headquarters of the Iranian 81st Armoured Division in Kermanshah Province, Iran. It is one of the tanks supplied to Iran in the late 1970s before the overthrow of the Shah. (photos: Vorya Heidaryan)

1, 2 The M60A1 is remarkably well preserved and stands alongside other AFVs from the Iran-Iraq War, both US-supplied Iranian material and captured Soviet-supplied Iraqi vehicles.

3 A close-up of the turret shows the cast texture and weld seams.

4, 5 The rubberised fabric mantlet cover and the mounting posts for the searchlight.

6 The heavy cast texture is also evident on M19 commander's cupola.

7, 8 The rear stowage basket. Note the tie-down points to secure the equipment stored here.

9 A close-up of the rear travel lock.

10 The distinctive headlights. Note the bolt detail of the headlight guard and fender support.

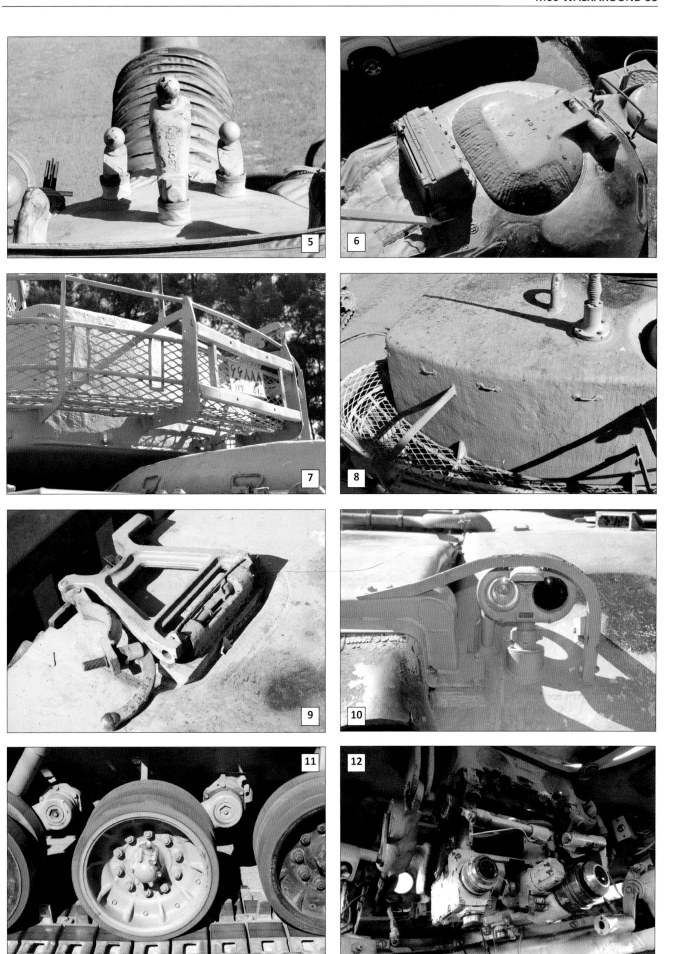

11 The ribbed aluminium roadwheels were used on all M60 models until they were replaced with steel ones in 1980. The M60A1s still in US service were frequently retrofitted with the new style roadwheels.

12 A view inside the M19 cupola and of the commander's M17C Coincidence Range Finder which offered x10 vision for both sighting and ranging potential targets.

M60 IN ACTION: THE COLD WAR

As the first new M60 Main Battle Tanks arrived in Germany in late 1960 the Cold War was entering a new deadly phase. The Soviet Union was closing 'the Missile Gap' and developing a nuclear arsenal with the potential to target American cities. In East Germany ten tank and ten motorised rifle divisions, with another 74 stationed west of the Urals and 35 divisions from its Warsaw Pact allies, stood ready to take on NATO's conventional forces. NATO's General Defence Plan of 1961 acknowledged that to have any chance of a sustained defence of Western Europe the Alliance would have to take the initiative in the deployment of nuclear weapons. The US Army's Seventh Army formed the bulk of the NATO's Central Army Group (CENTAG) and was divided between the V (US) Corps and VII (US) Corps. They had responsibility for the so-called Fulda Gap, one of the two obvious main axes of advance for any Soviet invasion of West Germany. By the end of 1963 all the Armor and Armored Cavalry battalions in US Seventh Army, except for those assigned to the Berlin Brigade, had replaced their M48 Pattons with the M60. Nevertheless, in the early 1960s the US Army was ill-prepared for mounting an effective conventional defence of West Germany as the so-called Pentomic divisional structure of the late 1950s had assumed a battlefield dominated by nuclear weapons.

By 1965 the US Army had adopted a new structure of three brigades per division, each with three, occasionally four, battalions per brigade. Each division had a mixture of armoured and infantry battalions that could mixed up as the operational situation demanded at the discretion of the divisional commander. New weapon systems, such as the Shillelagh ATGM, the Redeye shoulder-fired surface-to-air missile, and a new nuclear shell for the 155mm howitzer marked the end of the age of the 280mm atomic cannon and the Davy Crocket tactical nuclear weapon in favour of the doctrine of Flexible Response and a new emphasis on challenging the Warsaw Pact's conventional supremacy. This manifested itself in a re-evaluation of the importance of field training exercises. Although this had been evident since the early 1960s, it reached its apogee in the annual REFORGER (Return of Forces to Germany) exercises, first held in 1969.

The origins of the REFORGER exercises were in President Lyndon Johnson's decision in 1968 to withdraw two US divisions from Germany due to the escalation of the Vietnam War. To demonstrate the US's continuing commitment to NATO, an annual military exercise would take place that would involve the rapid transfer of at least a divisional-sized force from the United States to Germany and a field training exercise that committed these forces against other US and NATO forces. In wartime an entire third US corps, III (US) Corps, based at Fort Hood, Texas, and including two armoured divisions, a mechanised infantry division, and an Armored Cavalry regiment would be deployed to Germany, drawing tanks and other equipment from POMCUS depots in Belgium, the Netherlands, and West Germany.

The end of Vietnam War left the US Army disillusioned and broken. This was felt in USAEUR, where many junior and middle-ranking officers in particular had lost confidence in their commanders. As well as the end of the Vietnam War and the subsequent end of the draft, other factors occasioned a rethink of US Amy doctrine. First, the 1973 Yom Kippur War had shown how effective a small, well-trained force with good morale could be against a numerically and technologically superior opponent. Second, the death of the Army Chief of Staff, General Creighton Abrams, who had overseen the war in Vietnam, meant an inevitable change in focus and personnel in the Army's command. Efforts to revitalise the Army emphasised a new rigorous training programme for all levels of the new all-volunteer army and efforts to improve the effectiveness of small units. The early 'seventies also witnessed a heated argument over a new operational doctrine for the US Army. In July 1976 a new Army operational manual, FM-1005, was published which enshrined the notion of Active Defence and aligned the US Army's doctrine with that of its most important NATO partner, West Germany. In Europe, the US Army would use its skill to conduct a forward defence, based on manoeuvre and the concentrated application of force to fight and win against the Soviets. When General Don Starry, one of the architects of the new doctrine, was appointed commander of the V (US) Corps in 1976, he discovered an officer corps ill-equipped to put his ideas into practice. He instituted a practice of regular terrain walks, encouraging his divisional, brigade and battalion commanders to imagine the ground where they would engage and defeat the first echelon of the Soviet attack. Thus, in the late 1970s the M60s of the Amor and Armored Cavalry battalions of the Seventh Army took on a new importance as the spearhead of a conventional force that, for the first time, began to imagine defeating the Warsaw Pact in battle. They were deployed according to the notion of 'Forward Defense' close to the Inner German Border and designed to meet and destroy the massed Soviet armour as it poured through the Fulda Gap.

In the late 'seventies and early 'eighties, however, it was clear US operational plans in the event of a major Soviet invasion were insufficient. They were simply not enough reserves, and not enough tanks, to defeat the second and third echelons and eventually resort would have to be made to nuclear weapons. In 1982 the manual was revised by a younger team of officers in the US and the emphasis shifted away from direct firepower to one of offensive manoeuvre and surprise, designed to put

An M60A3 of 3-68 Armor, 8th (US) Infantry Division, crosses a Class 60 Medium Girder Bridge during Exercise Confident Enterprise, the field training component of REFORGER 83. (US National Archives)

the invader on the wrong foot and inflict a series of defeats in the so-called 'Deep Battle' doctrine. An integral part of this was the use of airpower, both strategic and tactical, to attack the Soviet second and third echelons and degrade their ability to fight and win against the armoured and mechanised infantry formations of Seventh Army. Another important component of this emerging doctrine were the successors to the M60 and M113 Armoured Personnel Carrier, the M1 Abrams MBT and the Bradley Fighting Vehicle. This new doctrine of the 'Airland Battle' envisaged a battle that would be fought and won in West Germany, as well as in East Germany and other central and Eastern European states and across the supply lines of the invading Soviet forces.

The AirLand Battle was adopted as the principal battle plan of the NATO forces in West Germany in 1984, just as the M60 was being phased out from frontline units. Importantly though, in the mid 1980s the M60 and its crews proved themselves capable of adapting to this new warfighting doctrine and the tank remained an effective weapon right up until its final withdrawal from Seventh Army in the last days of the Cold War. During the Field Training Exercise component of REFORGER 1985, 'Central Guardian', among the 'Blue' Forces all the armoured regiments of the 8th

(US) Infantry Division were still equipped with the M60 and only the 11th Armored Cavalry Regiment operated the M1 Abrams. Similarly, among the 'Orange Forces', only 3-68 Armor of 3rd (US) Armored Division had M1 Abrams, with the other four Armor battalions and one Cavalry battalion having M60A3. By the time of Exercise Certain Strike in September 1987, the then largest deployment of US forces during peacetime, the balance had been reversed but M60A3s were still drawn from POMCUS depots to equip 3-68 Armor which had deployed from Fort Carson, Colorado. The following year, during Exercise Certain Challenge, the M60A3 deployed for the final time in the REFORGER exercises.

Another interesting example of the effectiveness of the M60 in the early 1980s comes from the Canadian Army Trophy in 1983. In the summer of that year a team of M60A1 RISE from 2-68 Armor went head-to-head in a gunnery contest with M1 Abrams and Leopard 1s. The M60A1 came third, just behind the M1 Abrams of 3-64 Armor and a team of German Leopards. An analysis of the competition published later that year in Armor magazine stressed the reliability and accuracy of the M68 gun, but, above all else, the rigorous training and skill of the M60A1 crew that allowed them to compete on equal terms with the most modern of Main Battle Tanks.

An Iranian M60A1 of 231st Tank Battalion, 92nd Armoured Division, in Khuzestan Province, Iran, during the opening battles of the Iran-Iraq War. (Vorya Heidaryan)

M60 IN ACTION: THE MIDDLE EAST

While the guns of American M60s largely remained quiet during the Cold War, the same could not be said of those tanks exported to the United States' Middle Eastern friends and allies. The experience of the M60 in Israeli and Iranian service demonstrated the tank's shortcomings and provided important lessons for US armour doctrine. In 1973 the recently arrived 150 M60A1 represented a small fraction of Israel's total tank force of 2,138 vehicles. Almost half of these were Centurions, the majority upgraded to have the same diesel engine as the M60. The M60A1 was deployed in two Israeli reserve units, the 600th Armored Brigade and the 87th Reconnaissance Battalion, when the Syrians and Egyptians launched their attack on 6 October that year. They were deployed to the Sinai Peninsula as the M60's tracks were considered unsuitable for the terrain in the Golan Heights. The Egyptian attack across the Suez Canal caught the Israelis unprepared and in the first three days of the war they lost some 250 tanks to enemy action. On 14 October the Egyptians launched a major armoured assault. The M60A1s of 87th Reconnaissance Battalion were among the forces standing in their path and they inflicted heavy losses on the Egyptians. The following day the Israelis counterattacked with 87th Reconnaissance Battalion leading 14th Armored Brigade, now done to about a third of its original strength. During the Battle of the Chinese Farm on 17 October, the M60A1s crews demonstrated their superior training and fire control, successfully engaging the Egyptian T-62s at ranges of up to 2,000m. At the Chinese Farm the Egyptians lost 85 of their 96 T-62s for only four M60A1s destroyed on the Israeli side. The following day the Israeli M60s secured a bridgehead over the Canal, allowing their forces to pour into Africa, advancing to within 100km of Cairo before the war was brought to an end on 25 October.

The Israeli experience of the M60 during the Yom Kippur War was a mixed one. While relatively few were destroyed by enemy action, the tank proved less resilient than other makes in the IDF arsenal. A post-war report commissioned by the USMC found that while 60 per cent of the damaged Israeli Centurions and 55 per cent of their T-54/55s were repaired and returned to action during the war, only nineteen per cent of their M48s and M60s were similarly repaired. The M60 also gained an unfortunate reputation for catastrophic fires caused by the burning hydraulic fluid 'cooking off' the ammunition stored in the turret. Its additional height was also disliked by the Israelis and its M19 cupola was considered next to useless. During and immediately after the Yom Kippur War hundreds of additional M60s were sent to Israel, but these would undergo an extensive programme of modification before they satisfied the needs of the IDF. The Israeli commanders considered that it was not superior technology that had seen them prevail against the Egyptians in Sinai but the motivation, morale, experience and training of the Israeli crews. These were lessons that were not lost, as we have seen, on US planners in the wake of the Yom Kippur War.

The other principal user of the M60 in the Middle East was, of course, Iran. By the time of the Iran-Iraq War in September 1980, the M60A1 had been supplanted by the British Chieftain Mk. 5 as the most potent tank in Iran's arsenal. Nevertheless, on the eve of war eight battalions of M60A1s (each with 53 tanks) served in the 81st Armoured Division in the west of the country, two with the 92nd Armoured Division and another two with the 37th Armoured Brigade in southern Iran. In the first Iranian attack near the city of Bostan in Khuzestan Province, the high profile of the M60A1 proved an easy target for Iraqi ATGM teams. Similarly, in the flat desert around the city of Khorramshahr the 92nd Armoured Division suffered heavy losses to Iraqi ATGMs. Further north on the western border of the Meimack region, the M60A1s of the 81st Armoured Division were able

to engage Iraqi armour more successfully at long range in the mountainous terrain. In 1981 the Iranians counterattacked but in the Battle of Dezful they suffered heavy losses as their tanks became bogged down in the marshy ground. Increasingly, the M60A1s were held in reserve, while the Chieftains, with their more powerful L11 120mm gun, took on the Iraqi T-62s and T-72s. In May the following year M60A1s played a full part in the major tank battle at Shalmche, where the Iranian crews prevailed by means of their superior long-range gunnery, leading to the liberation of the Iranian city of Khorramshahr.

After the liberation of Khorramshahr, Iranian tactics changed and refined combined arms operations were abandoned in favour of bloody 'human wave' assaults. The M60A1s of the Iranian Army saw

(above) A battle worn M60A1 of 237th Tank Battalion, 37th Armoured Brigade, photographed near the city of Abadan, Iran, in 1981. Note the improvised sandbag armour around the turret and the national insignia on the fender stowage bin. (Vorya Heidaryan)

relatively little action as the course of the war was increasingly prosecuted by the Revolutionary Guard and Basij volunteer forces. Nevertheless, the Iran-Iraq War taught similar lessons on the effectiveness of the M60 to those that had emerged in 1973. First, the high profile of the M60 left it vulnerable to ATGMs. Second, its M68 gun and ammunition were superior to those of Soviet-designed tanks at long range. Third, and most importantly, the experience of the M60 in the Iran-Iraq War again underlined the paramount importance of crew morale and training.

Another Iranian M60A1 of 92nd Armoured Division in 1981. (Vorya Heidaryan)

An USMC M60A1 (RISE Passive) guards the Marine Corps' barrack near Beirut International Airport in April 1983, just months before the bomb blast that killed 241 US military personnel there. (USMC photo by Gunnery Sgt. R.D. Lucas)

M60 IN ACTION: OTHER US ACTIONS

The only offensive action in which US M60s were involved during the Cold War was Operation Urgent Fury, the US-led invasion of Grenada in October 1993. The operation was designed to topple the Communist People's Revolutionary Government after the murder of the previous leader, Prime Minister Maurice Bishop. US Marines from the 22nd Marine Assault Unit, equipped with four M60A1 tanks, landed at Mal Bay on 25 October. They pushed inland amid sporadic resistance, destroying a BRDM-2 armoured car, and freed the Governor-General, Sir Paul Goodwin Scoon. At the same time, USMC M60A1s were also deployed with 1st Battalion, 8th Marine Regiment, as part of the Multinational Force in Lebanon, designed to bring peace to that war-ravaged country.

US M60s also continued to serve on the Korean Peninsula during the Cold War. Here a USMC M60A1 (RISE Passive) comes ashore during Exercise Team Spirit 82. (USN photo by PH1 Dennis Brockschmidt)

M60 IN ACTION: THE FIRST GULF WAR

As the Cold War in Europe drew to its conclusion, the M60 found itself engaged in a very different theatre to one in which it was initially designed to operate in. On 2 August 1990 Iraqi forces invaded Kuwait. Within 48 hours the Emir had fled, the Kuwaiti armed forces had either surrendered or escaped to Saudi Arabia, and a coalition of nations, led by the United States, was organising to demand the Iraqis withdraw from what Saddam Hussein would soon declare 'the nineteenth province of Iraq'. The invasion had been planned long in advance and the warning signs largely ignored by the Kuwaitis and their allies. At the time Iraq had the fourth largest army in the world and their soldiers had recent combat experience in the long and bloody Iran-Iraq War, which had ended just two years previously. Nevertheless, by the end of February 1991 the Iraqi army had been effectively destroyed and the invaders had been thrown out of Kuwait in ignominious defeat. The ground campaign, which lasted just one hundred hours, was the swansong of the M60 but one in which it again proved itself an effective MBT.

In the aftermath of the Iraqi invasion of Kuwait the US quickly reinforced Saudi Arabia with armour. Among the first American tanks to arrive in the Gulf were the M60A3 TTS of 2-69 Armor and 4th Cavalry Regiment, both part of the 24th Infantry (Mechanized) Division. These tanks remained with the US Army for a short period before they were replaced with M1 Abrams and the M60s transferred to the USMC's 1st and 3rd Tank Battalions. The other US M60A3s that saw service in the first Gulf War did so with the US Air Force and were used on airbases in the unexploded ordnance role, using a M9 dozer blade to push unexploded ordnance to safety.

The M60 was the principal MBT of the United States Marine Corps during the First Gulf War. In 1st Marine Division the M60A1 (RISE Passive) equipped 1st and 3rd Tank Battalions; in 2nd Marine Division the reservists of 8th Tank Battalion were similarly equipped; two companies of 4th Tank Battalion, another reservist unit, also had M60A1s. Two companies of 8th Tank Battalion and 2nd Tank Battalion were equipped with the M1A1 Abrams. The Marine Corps had been reluctant to adopt the heavier, gas-turbine engine Abrams as they considered it less suited to amphibious warfare, while the 120mm gun of the M1A1 lacked a high explosive and canister round capability at the time of the First Gulf War. The first M60A1s arrived in theatre on 17 August 1990, days after the Marine tankers, and were unloaded from their Maritime Prepositioning Ships (MPS). These tanks were new and unused, and the crews quickly had to bring them to combat readiness and learn to use the Discarding Sabot ammunition that the USMC had not fired in peacetime. Other tanks, such as those that equipped the 8th Tank Battalion, were shipped over from reserves held at Camp Lejeune, North Carolina. The tanks were also fitted with their ERA armour at Al Jubyal by civilian contractors from Anniston Army Depot, Alabama, and received a coat of Desert Tan paint over their various MERDC and NATO camouflage finishes. By the middle of September, however, the USMC tank battalions were ready and had taken their place among the Coalition forces guarding Saudi Arabia. Alongside the Marine Corps' M60s, the Saudi and Egyptian forces also deployed large numbers of M60A3 during

'Lefty', an M60A1 (RISE Passive) of 1st Tank Battalion, surrounded by the camp beds of its crew in Saudi Arabia during Operation Desert Storm. (US National Archives)

This M60A1 (RISE Passive) of Company C, 8th Tank Battalion, is fitted with a Pearson Mine Plough, a vital piece of equipment in making the initial advance into Kuwait. (Greg Smith)

Operation Desert Shield.

There were some concerns over the serviceability and effectiveness of the USMC's M60A1 compared to newer US Army's Abrams. In the early weeks of Operation Desert Shield, for instance, large numbers of the Saudi M60A3s were rendered inoperable because of clogged air filters, although that had been rectified by the time they played an important role in defeating the Iraqi incursion at the battle of Khafji on 29 January 1991. The tanks drawn from the MPS and from Camp Lejeune were in varying degrees of readiness, some were missing parts including batteries, sights and rangefinders, and ammunition was in short supply. More serious was the shortage of fuel. CENTCOM had decided to supply only high-quality jet fuel, which the older M60A1s, used to running on diesel, struggled with. Oil had to be added to the fuel for it to work properly, and fuel filters quickly became one of the most sought after items in the desert. Another issue was the Army M60A3s scattered among the USMC battalions, with their new thermal sight. Some USMC tankers expressed fears about the superior long-range capability of the Iraqi T-72s. One observed: 'The only thing we've got to do is when they come, we've got to get close with them right away and take away the advantage they have in outgunning us. In close, we'll have more maneuverability, we'll have the sabot round, and we'll cause some problems.'

Conditions in the desert were tough as the Marine Corps tankers awaited the next move in the war. Sickness and diarrhoea, caused by eating local fresh produce, was a frequent problem, as were the dangers of dehydration. The desert winter was also wet and cold and supplies of heavy sleeping bags were brought to the USMC tank battalions from the camp at Twentynine Palms, California. The M60A1s began to suffer under the harsh conditions with fuel lines wearing out becoming an issue.

By the end of January 1991, the USMC's role in the forthcoming battle for the liberation of Kuwait was becoming clearer. In 1st Marine Division's southern section of the front the two tank-heavy formations, Task Forces RIPPER and PAPA BEAR, would lead the attack, breaching the Iraqi sand berm and minefield defences. To this end, full-width mine ploughs were issued to each tank platoon, while 1st Tank Battalion also used 'roller dude', an improvised mine roller device, as well as Israeli-supplied mine rollers. M60A1s also towed trailer-mounted mine clearing devices. By the time the offensive started two M60A1s in each platoon were equipped with ploughs, rakes or rollers of some description. 2nd Marine Division, augmented by the Abrams of the Army's 1st (Tiger) Brigade, 2nd Armored Division, was tasked with entering Kuwait from the north. With 257 tanks, 2nd Marine Division was the most powerful armoured formation ever fielded by the USMC.

Nevertheless, on the eve of battle, some Marines were a little unsure of the role assigned to them. One tanker recalled that while the Army formations of VII Corps would make a classic armoured advance across the open desert into Iraq, 'we were going straight up the middle [into Kuwait]. There was no maneuver, straight up the gut here ... We got the tanks with the least amount of armor, we can't see at night, we don't have the latest in range-finding gear. It was kind of like "This is crazy!"'

At 0400 on Sunday, 24 February 1991, the tanks of Task Force RIPPER entered the Iraqi minefields and began the push into Kuwait. Predictably, no plan ever goes smoothly and soon the advance was being delayed by explosive line charges, designed to blast a path through the minefield, failing to detonate, while inevitably some tanks were damaged and had to be recovered under sporadic Iraqi artillery fire and the constant danger of unexploded mines. In 2nd Marine Division's area of operations, 2nd Tank Battalion had opened a path through the minefield by 1250 for the Abrams of the

Tiger Brigade to pour through.

As it turned out, the fears of the USMC tankers were unfounded and their M60A1s proved more than capable of engaging and destroying the Iraqi armour. 3rd Tank Battalion, for instance, soon realised that most of the dug-out enemy tanks they came across were unmanned. When they did engage the Iraqi armour with discarding sabot ammunition, the rounds went straight through the armour of the T-55s and T-62s, destroying everything and anyone inside. One 3rd Tank Battalion commander recounted: 'The smoke clouds from burning oil wells were closing in fast, reducing visibility to less than 1,500 meters. All of a sudden my loader, Lance Corporal Rodrigues, yelled: "We got a T-62 out there – look!"'. The M60A1 fired a sabot round at 1,100 metres range and 'the first explosion was small but then its ammo started cooking off'. Fourteen secondary explosions were counted, completely destroying the Iraqi tank.

On the morning of 25 February, the Iraqis launched their counterattack against the M60A1s of 1st Tank Battalion, Task Force PAPA BEAR. Two Iraqi brigades attacked the USMC positions in the al-Burqan oilfield. The battle raged for some three hours, with the USMC tanks joined by the attack helicopters and HMMWV-mounted TOWs, in routing the Iraqi forces, with Company C, 1st Tank Battalion, destroying eighteen enemy tanks in the process. The battle was joined at ranges of only some 500m, the limits of the M60A1s' passive sights, and

the dangers of fratricide were managed by the Marines' superior gunnery schools and their ability to shoot before their Iraqi counterparts. In all fifty Iraqi tanks and 22 APCs were knocked out for no American losses. 2nd Marine Division's tanks fared just as well: in the defensive position known as the 'Ice Tray' M60A1s of 8th Tank Battalion destroyed thirteen enemy tanks despite the poor visibility forcing the crews to rely on their conventional M32 battlesights.

The 26 February was the final day of combat for the USCM M60A1s and followed a familiar pattern. 1st Tank Battalion knocked out a further fifty tanks and 25 APCs, while 3rd Tank Battalion claimed 62 tank kills. 8th Tank Battalion accounted for over thirty destroyed enemy tanks. The lack of night sights meant that most of these engagements took place in daylight and at ranges of less than 1,000 metres, although an M60A3 attached to 1st Tank Battalion claimed a kill at 3,200 metres. The Iraqi tanks had no defence against the Marine tanks' discarding sabot rounds. One officer from 3rd Tank Battalion described the effect of the 105mm APDS round on the armour of a T-72: 'One round hit the frontal arc of the turret of a T-72. It went through the turret, engine, then out the ass-end.' By comparison no M60s were lost to or even hit by Iraqi tanks. Ten USMC tanks were lost in the initial mine-clearing operation, five of those fitted with ploughs or mine rakes. Ultimately, the M60A1 prevailed over its opponent because of the superior training and gunnery of the USMC crewmen.

One of 8th Tank Battalion's M60A1s damaged during the crossing of the minefield into Kuwait. (Greg Smith)

Further Reading

The standard technical of history of the M60, and its Patton tank predecessors, remains R.P. Hunnicutt, *Patton: A History of the American Main Battle Tank, Volume 1* (Presidio Press, 2015 edn.) This book chronicles the various prototypes of the M60 and the standard production variants and is well illustrated with photographs and technical drawings. The title by Richard Lathrop, *M60 Main Battle Tank 1960-91* (Osprey Publishing, 2003) in the Osprey New Vanguard series is a little light on technical details and history but has some useful insights. The best combination of technical and operational histories of the M60 series, as well as a collection of superb photographs, are the two volumes by Carl Schulze for Tankograd Publishing: *M60, M60A1 & M728* (Tankograd American Special, 3021) and *M60A2, M60A3 & AVLB* (Tankograd American Special, 3022). A good collection of photos of the M60 in Germany during the Cold War can be found in Walter Böhm, *Cold War Warrior: M60/M60A1/A2/A3* (Tankograd American Special, 3030). An interesting discussion of the M60 in combat, both in American and Israeli service, is Lon Nordeen and David Isby, *M60 vs T-72: Cold War Combatants 1956-92* (Osprey Publishing, 2010), while Chris McNab's *Sagger Anti-Tank Missile vs M60 Main Battle Tank: Yom Kippur War 1973* (Osprey Publishing, 2017) looks at the fortunes of the Israeli-operated M60s during the 1973 war.

There are a number of photo albums available that will inform and inspire those modellers wishing to tackle an M60 project:

Yves Debay, *USMC Firepower: Armor & Artillery* (Concord Publications Company, 1990)

David Doyle, *M60 Main Battle Tank in Action* (Squadron Signal, 2017)

Michael Greer and Greg Stewart, *M60* (Concord Publications Company, 1992)

Jim Mesko, *M60 Patton in Action* (Squadron Signal, 1986)

Chris Mrosko et al, *M60A2 Main Battle Tank in Detail, Volumes 1 & 2* (Sabot Publications, 2016)

Chris Mrosko, *USMC M60A1 Warmachines No. 5 Photo Reference Book* (Sabot Publications, 2017)

Chris Mrosko et al, *M60A3 Main Battle Tank in Detail, Volume 1* (Sabot Publications, 2018)

François Verlinden et al, *M60A3 War-machines No. 3 Military Photo File* (Verlinden Productions, 1990)

Thanks to Mark Smith, David Chou, Federico Collada, Vorya Heidaryan, Uwe Kern, José Luis Lopez Ruiz, Chris Mrosko, MP Robinson, Carl Schulze, Greg Smith, Hans Stenzel, Sławomir Zajączkowski for contributing ideas, photographs and models to this volume. This volume would not have been possible without the resources of the US National Archives.

A New York Army National Guard M60A1 (RISE Passive), followed by an M48A5, of 1-210 Armor during Exercise Sentry Castle in 1981. Sentry Castle involved some 15,000 reservists and was the largest exercise of its kind held in the state of New York. (US Army photo by Sgt. Marvin D. Lynchard)